IN SEARCH OF
TRUTH

Eliza Harrison

The Book Guild Ltd

First published in Great Britain in 2023 by
The Book Guild Ltd
Unit E2 Airfield Business Park,
Harrison Road, Market Harborough,
Leicestershire. LE16 7UL
Tel: 0116 2792299
www.bookguild.co.uk
Email: info@bookguild.co.uk
Twitter: @bookguild

Typeset in 11pt Minion Pro

Printed and bound by CPI Group (UK) Ltd, Croydon, CR0 4YY

ISBN 978 1915603 654

British Library Cataloguing in Publication Data.
A catalogue record for this book is available from the British Library.

Front cover photo: John Vere Brown

To my grandchildren and great-granddaughter Shara,
my hope and inspiration for the future

ACKNOWLEDGEMENTS

~

As I journeyed into my past, I came across unexpected people who offered their help and support. Firstly, I would like to acknowledge my niece Branwen as without her I may never have discovered my true heritage. The same goes for Richard and Jean Wiseman, who showed sympathy and understanding as they guided me through ancestral sites, searching for leads and answers. I would also like thank Dan Smith, author of *The Peer and the Gangster* and his literary agent Andrew Lownie, who encouraged me to tell this story and gave me invaluable guidance while sketching out this book.

But a very special thank you goes to my editor Michael Worton, former Vice-Provost of University College London, who with insight and wisdom encouraged me to delve more deeply into myself and the meaning of truth.

As always, love and gratitude goes to my husband David, who consistently stands by my side throughout whatever crazy venture I embark upon; in this case tirelessly reading and re-reading text and suggesting changes. And lastly blessings to my new family, the Careys, Kennedys, Liz Foster-Hall and Katherine Calvocoressi, who all welcomed me into their homes and lives and shared stories about times past and present. You made me feel I belonged and for that I shall always be grateful.

Seeds of Fear

~

My father, or the person I believed to be my father, lifted me up out of bed and carried me outside in the middle of the night. I was little more than two years old.

'Look, Elizabeth. Never forget this.'

Above Rabbit Hill was a row of vast columns of spiralling white, yellow and gold light, cascading up and down in a brilliant blaze.

'What is it?' I asked sleepily.

'The Northern Lights – it's very rare to see them here.'

There were gasps of awe from other family members who were standing nearby.

'Who would think?' said my grandmother. 'Seeing the Northern Lights as far south as Cornwall.'

'Try and remember this, Elizabeth,' my father said with tenderness in his voice, 'you may never see them again.'

And the image of radiance, beauty and wonder stayed with me, serving as a reminder of how light can miraculously explode from the dark.

I clung to this memory as seeds of fear were sown early – in my highchair when I was presented with a fried egg that was burned underneath. I stared at it, unable to bring a piece to my mouth.

'Eat up, Elizabeth,' my mother said in a sharp voice.

I remained silent.

'Do as you're told.'

I did not move.

My mother raised her voice: 'Eat it, I said.'

I shook my head.

Then my mother grabbed a teaspoon and attempted to force-feed me, but I kept my mouth tight shut. The thought of eating the egg that was cold and leathery made me feel sick. Then the tirade began. All I could hear were shrieks and screams as no words were decipherable. At one point I looked up and saw her reddened face as she shook her fists above her head. Her voice penetrated every part of me. But I was strapped into my highchair and there was no escape. I put my hands over my face so I could not see her, but her screams seared through me. She was uncontrollable, crazed. And it was just about an egg. The outburst went on and on, until finally I heard the words.

'You'll not forget this.'

And she grabbed me under my arms, pulled me out of the highchair and thrust me down in my playpen before going out of the room and slamming the door behind her. Alone, silence and the safety of my playpen bars, along with the recognition that life would be easier if I did as I was told.

At the time we lived in Cambridge, opposite a pub, a mill pond and the fens. My parents, Dick and Nora David, moved in a circle of distinguished academics and socialised regularly. Dinner and tennis parties, croquet on the lawn, a martini or Manhattan before supper were all options. My mother was the organiser and my father followed along. Everyone liked him as he was gracious, kind and had a wide range of interests that included music, art, literature and flowers. I rarely saw him as he worked in London at the sales office of the Cambridge University Press and, when he came home at weekends, he needed time to recuperate. He gardened, listened to Bach, carved the Sunday joint and on rare occasions took us for a walk. When I got tired he lifted me on his shoulders, which took me into another world. From up high, I had a different perspective of people and my surroundings, and momentarily felt apart from the fray. But physically, this was the closest I got to my father. I can never remember him taking me on his knee, reading me a story or playing any games with me.

I found other ways to have fun. I was physically agile and loved to compete, so my two older brothers and sister made up endless games to play.

My favourite expression was: 'S'all I?', and with a nod of approval from whoever was around, I would climb higher up the willow tree, swim in the river without a rubber ring and persist in riding a two-wheeler bike despite repeatedly falling off. But sometimes the risks I took were too great. When I was standing and then sitting on the swing, I missed my footing and fell awkwardly. My father was in the garden, heard my screams and saw me writhing about on the ground. Excruciating pain shot through my leg. He picked me up carefully, took me inside and called my mother, who was alarmed.

'It's probably broken. I'll take her to hospital.'

With a fracture confirmed and my leg plastered from foot to thigh, life was put on hold. It was then that I realised that whenever I was poorly, my mother's mood changed. She showed kindness and care and looked after me in a way she found difficult to do when I was well.

And my mother was always in a good mood whenever Bob Boothby came to stay. He was my sister Teresa's godfather and adored her, but he always made sure that I was included too. He was generous, fun-loving and made us laugh. He had a twinkle in his eye, as though he knew something that we did not.

'Pussy cats,' he said, embracing us. 'I've brought you some presents from France.'

Proudly he presented us each with two beautifully wrapped boxes. Thrilled to have gifts when it was not Christmas, we opened our parcels to find two red and white pinafore dresses, different from any I had seen before. I put mine on and felt grown-up and pretty. And when my mother's back was turned, Bob slid us both a bar of Dairy Milk chocolate and whispered, 'Keep that for yourselves.'

So I hid mine in my bedside drawer and had two squares a day to make it last.

The household relaxed when Bob was around. It was a time that I knew my mother would not get cross, so for a while I was on reprieve. There was a feeling of ease and lightness as Bob regaled us with stories about well-known people and goings-on in parliament. In return my mother treated him to the best of her cooking – paprika cod garnished with grapes, and roast lamb with all the trimmings – and the meals were always accompanied by a bottle of hock or Beaujolais that Bob had brought. When my father was home, I noticed how Bob carefully steered the conversation to the latest opera or concert he had seen to ensure he was included. Not having a family of his own, Bob relaxed in the company of ours and fitted in seamlessly.

'Would you like me to make a French omelette?' he asked. 'I was taught by the chef in one of best restaurants in Monte Carlo.'

Delighted to have Bob's help in the kitchen, my mother passed him the omelette pan, butter and a mixing bowl. First he whisked the eggs, adding salt and pepper, then lit the gas on a low flame and waited for the butter to melt. When it was slightly foaming, with an exaggerated gesture, he poured the eggs into the pan allowing the mixture to cover the base.

'Only when the bottom is just set do you gently draw the mixture to one side… like this.'

And with precision he took the spatula, tilted the pan, drew the mixture to one side and allowed the remaining liquid to cover the bottom of the pan. He repeated this once more before folding the omelette and serving it on two plates for Teresa and me.

'There you are – an authentic French omelette. Enjoy it, my treasures.'

I savoured the first mouthful, allowed it to dissolve in my mouth and could truthfully say it was the best omelette I had ever eaten.

Bob was not only generous with Teresa and me, but my parents too. Besides a washing machine and other household gifts, he gave us a car, which meant my mother could drive us to my grandmother's house in Cornwall where we spent every summer holiday. She had a house above a sandy bay that overlooked a National Trust headland with sheer cliffs and hidden coves. Days were spent on a beach, where we would swim, surf, scramble on the rocks and search for cowrie shells. But despite being on holiday, I was always wary of my mother's moods.

'Get in the water, Elizabeth.'

'It's too rough,' I replied.

We were on a beach where getting into the sea entailed scrambling over rocks, encrusted with barnacles that hurt my feet. There was also a bitter wind, the sea was choppy and I did not feel sufficiently confident to cope with the waves.

'You didn't come to Cornwall to sit on a beach. Go for a swim,' she commanded.

'But it's freezing.'

'Get in,' she said again. 'That's what we've come for.'

At this point I was shivering from fear as well as cold, so I got into my swimsuit and tiptoed my way over the rocks towards the water.

'Go on,' she shouted again.

So in I went, gulping in seawater as I choked on my tears.

I resented being treated differently from my siblings. One of my brothers only swam when he felt like it and he was never reprimanded. My sister Teresa was able to opt out too. So why was I the one who was singled out? I could not even appeal to my father. When he did come to Cornwall, he rarely came on days out but preferred to spend his time alone, botanising, foraging for food, and at low tide scouring the rock pools and crevices for crabs and the occasional lobster. Then with his hook he would prise it out, check if it was big enough to eat before bringing his catch home for my mother to cook and shell. But he did accompany us the day I was running down Rabbit Hill and fell into a gorse bush. When we got home it was my father who, with magnifying glass and tweezers in hand, meticulously took out every thorn as I stood naked on the lawn. And although it took a while, I did not mind as at last I had his undivided attention.

Although my father lived in a world of his own, at least I felt safe as he never scolded me. But there was one time he told me off and I was shaken to the core. I was at the bottom of the garden, forking the compost pile, pretending it was hay for my make-believe horses.

'Elizabeth, don't do that,' he shouted from an upstairs window.

I looked up in disbelief that he was talking to me in this way, dropped the fork and ran away. It was not the reprimand that I minded, but the fact that it was from my father, who never seemed to get angry.

So my early childhood was spent navigating an uncertain path between my mother's irascibility and my father's indifference. Going to stay with Victor and Tess Rothschild, whose daughter Emma was the same age as me, should have offered some reprieve but instead it felt like banishment. Each time I was told that a visit had been arranged, familiar feelings arose. Pain in my gut and a lump in my throat that I could not release through crying as tears were not allowed. At least when I was home, there was always hope that things might change. Maybe my mother's anger would dissipate and my father would begin to play with me? So whenever I was sent away, feelings of abandonment and rejection intensified.

The regime began when I was less than two years old and continued throughout my childhood. Although Victor and Tess were kind and welcoming, each time I went to stay at Merton Hall I became desperately homesick. I would lie awake at night and wonder if I could find my way home along the backs of the colleges. But I knew there were alarms in their seventeenth-century timber-framed house, so there was no escape. Instead I cried silently, wondering if this nightmare would ever end.

My mother had been at university with Tess and since then, the Rothschilds had become my parents' closest friends. Tess was my godmother, a responsibility that she undertook with diligence and care. But I noticed that there was a nervousness about her that was expressed in a facial twitch. It was Victor who commanded the attention. He never failed to make his presence felt no matter who was around. But I never felt in awe of him as he always made a point of including me. When he emerged from his study, he would jest, comment on a game I was playing or ask some surprising question. It felt as though Victor was testing me, curious to find out more about me.

One day he followed me into the garden and said, 'I've got a new name for you.'

I looked at him quizzically. 'But my name's Elizabeth.'

He paused for a moment and then said, 'Your new name's Biff Squeal.'

'Biff Squeal,' I exclaimed. 'Why?'

'Because your mother biffs you and then you squeal.'

'But I don't,' I retorted, knowing that I always tried to hide the hurt.

'So we'll just call you Biff then,' Victor affirmed.

From then on I became Biff to everyone apart from my parents, who continued to call me Elizabeth, and the name stayed with me until I left school. I did not like it, but I did not resent Victor for giving it to me as it seemed as though he wanted to make a point about the way my mother treated me.

I knew that she found it challenging bringing up four children. Sometimes I wondered why she had a family at all. She was more interested in socialising and pursuing her political career. But she was wedded to convention, cared about what others thought and so the family status was important to her. As my brothers went to preparatory school when they were eight years old, my mother only had Teresa and me to look after. Nevertheless she relied upon a succession of au pairs for help – Thérèse, Ella and Giuditta – but none of them lasted long. Her standards were high and she lost her temper if a job was not done right. There were language problems too. But everything changed when Joan arrived. She had been recommended by a friend as being conscientious and reliable, even though she was only fifteen years old. And unlike the other au pairs, Joan wanted to learn how to lay a table, iron my father's shirts, clean the silver and was unafraid of my mother's anger. She was also able to assess the family dynamics and see if something was amiss. So she sympathised when she saw that I was the one who got the blame when it was my sister who had misbehaved. Now Joan was there to protect me.

When the weather was inclement and we were banished from the house for the obligatory afternoon walk, she made sure that we did not get wet and cold.

'We'll go to the Fitzwilliam Museum,' she suggested. 'It'll be warm and dry in there.'

'Can we look at the armour?' I asked.

Joan knew that I loved staring at these metal men and imagining them riding into battle on white chargers.

'If they were real, would they fight for me?' I asked.

'There's no need. I'm here for you now.'

'Not when I go to the Rothschilds.'

'The angels will protect you there.'

'I've never seen them.'

'When I want help, I ask them to come and my worries float away,' Joan said convincingly.

My parents never talked about God or angels, but I felt Joan was telling the truth and that there might be little winged creatures around who were there to look after me. But whether they existed or not, at least I had Joan. A knee to sit on, a hand to hold, someone that I could reach out to when I wanted to be consoled. I always felt safe with Joan.

MERTON HALL

~

I noticed I was being sent to my room more than usual. Not that I had done anything wrong. It seemed my parents wanted time alone and I was not privy to grown-up conversations. I relied upon Joan to tell me what was going on.

'We're moving,' she said as I was getting into bed.

'Why?' I asked.

'This house belongs to Corpus Christi College and they want it back.'

The idea of change disturbed me and Joan could see I was perplexed.

'It's exciting,' she said encouragingly. 'We're going to see the new house tomorrow.'

'But I don't want to move.'

'We have no choice.'

For me, Ashton House gave me a sense of security whereas my family did not. The idea of losing it felt scary.

Dark red tiles in the hallway and dingy paint colours made a forbidding welcome to our new home. My first impression was that the house felt oppressive and its layout was confusing. It was on three floors with numerous side passages, disconnected rooms and the bathroom was through an attic room at the top of the house. Joan suggested we take a look around the garden instead.

'Look,' she said, pointing to a mature walnut tree, 'we can put the swing up there.'

But I found it difficult to summon up any enthusiasm.

'They're going to redecorate,' Joan reassured me. 'The house will feel completely different when that's done. And I'm sure we can persuade your mother to give you and Teresa a room on the first floor.'

'It'll be further to bike to school,' I said, 'and winter's coming so it'll be cold.'

'It's less than two miles and I'll be with you.'

But school was a challenge too. I had been at Byron House for just over a year and was having difficulty fitting in. I guessed it was because I was small and prone to getting bullied. Strangely it was my agility that got me into most trouble. I was chivvied into having a race with a girl in my class, who was popular and everyone's favourite to win. I realised from the beginning it was not going to turn out well. I would be jeered at if I lost and resented if I won.

'Let's see how fast you can run,' taunted the girl's brother, throwing back his mop of ginger hair.

I got off to a good start and my legs were carrying me effortlessly. I glanced sideways and saw the other girl slipping behind. I was not going to hold back now. Seeing the finish line loom up in front of me, I bounded home and collapsed in a heap on the lawn. As I looked up, I saw the girl's brother glaring down at me.

'You cheated. We'll show you what happens to cheats. Come on, Mary.'

He and his sister pulled me towards a wooded area to one side of the playground where we could not be seen. Then the boy pulled out some string, tied me to a tree, and the pinching, scratching and punching began.

'Say you cheated and you're sorry,' the boy menaced.

I had no intention of submitting to their threats, nor did I want them to see me cry, so I gritted my teeth, uttered no words and shed no tears, and after a while they got bored.

'Come on, let's leave her. She's stupid anyway,' the boy said as they left.

And being called 'stupid' was what hurt the most as I believed it to be true.

The move to the new house was soon followed by a change of schools. Victor wanted to open a private school for Emma and I was invited to attend along with a handful of other pupils. I knew my mother would agree as her first priority was to please her friends. She explained that they had found an excellent teacher and the new school would be built in the grounds of Merton Hall.

'So is it already decided?' I asked.

'You'll have a first-class education and you're very lucky to have this opportunity.'

I had no choice but to accept the decision. But I was wary about being educated in close proximity to Emma. She was an avid reader, fast at arithmetic, had vast span of general knowledge and I would now be spending term times as well as the holidays at Merton Hall.

Shortly after the school opened, Victor appeared and told our teacher that he wanted to take the lesson. To my relief, he assured us that he would only be asking simple questions.

'What colour is the sea?' he began.

A few of us put up our hands.

'Biff,' he said, looking directly at me.

'Blue,' I answered.

'Anyone else?' he asked.

Emma volunteered, 'Transparent. Water is transparent and the sea takes on the colour of the sky.'

'Who do you think is right?' Victor asked the class. 'Is the sea the colour we perceive it to be, or the colour of water itself?'

There were murmurings among my classmates, before someone mentioned that the sea was blue when it is was sunny and grey when it is cloudy. So it was agreed that Emma had the correct answer.

'Next question, what's the colour of lipstick?'

This time I did not volunteer, sensing this would be another trap.

Someone called out 'red'.

'Just red?' Victor queried.

Once again, Emma put her hand up, saying there were different shades of red.

'It's true,' Victor confirmed. 'The colour red can range from dark pink to ruby. You see, nothing is as it seems to be.'

I was often aware that Victor was watching me. It was as though he was weighing me up, wondering how I fitted into my family, related to my mother, father and siblings. When there was an opportunity he liked to probe. On one occasion when I was with Victor, Tess and Emma in their drawing room with their friends Alan and Marni Hodgkin, he hushed everyone and asked me to stand in the middle of the room. Disliking being the centre of attention, I rose to my feet reluctantly.

'Tell us, Biff, how do you survive your mother?'

'What do you mean?'

'Your mother is very strict. How do you cope?'

Surprised by the question, I was unsure how to answer.

'She's the only mother I know,' I said quietly.

I was accustomed to Victor's unexpected questions, but this one took me by surprise. Maybe my mother's disciplinarian nature was unusual and it was discussed among her friends? As I glanced about the room, I noticed sympathy on the faces of those gathered, but my answer seemed to satisfy Victor so he did not question me further.

I knew that spending time with the Rothschilds broadened my horizons, so as I got older, I resented it less. I was not only a frequent visitor at Merton Hall but also Rushbrooke, their country home in Suffolk, an arable farm set amongst gently rolling countryside. Apart from its extensive wine cellars, the original manor house on the estate was now abandoned and a new home had been built. Surrounded by a mellow redbrick wall, the gardens comprised lawns, flowering shrubs, and through an archway was a market garden where an array of vegetables and exotic fruit were grown. And beyond a courtyard and stables, which led on to a country lane.

Tess managed the household seamlessly. In the morning she decided on menus with the kitchen staff, read the newspaper, wrote letters, entertained friends and under Victor's guidance agreed upon house guests that should be invited to stay. Meals took place in the dining room, and apart from formal dinner parties, Emma and I were always included. At breakfast, I helped myself from the hotplate and in the evening was waited upon by the butler. We were encouraged to taste everything. This was no problem if it was succulent peaches from the farm, but it was more difficult when it was a rich pâté, or the obligatory small glass of wine to 'develop our palate'. Unlike my mother, however, Tess and Victor embraced me as one of their own, accepting me for who I was, instead of judging me for who I was not.

We had freedom too. We were allowed to rag around in Victor and Tess's bedroom, build real dens with bricks and mortar, make fudge with Nana, and have dripping sandwiches. Tess also tried to find ways to make me feel more self-confident.

'Look, Biff, here's a book by your namesake, Elizabeth David.'

It was difficult to believe that someone with the same name as me had written a book.

'It's a recipe book,' Tess explained. 'She writes about the different ways that vegetables, fish and meat are cooked around the Mediterranean Sea.'

As she handed me the book, it felt strange seeing my name on the cover.

'Maybe one day you'll write a book,' Tess said encouragingly.

'I doubt it,' I replied, admiring the cover picture of a table with vegetables and a bottle of wine, set against a background of sea and sailing boats.

'It's a painting of the south of France,' Tess explained. 'We're planning a holiday there. Would you like to come?'

I was taken aback by the invitation, as to me, abroad and passports seemed far removed from family and school life in Cambridge.

'Me... really?'

'Of course.' Tess smiled.

And unexpectedly another opportunity opened up through the generosity of the Rothschilds.

My mother was pleased that her daughter had been invited to go to France with the Rothschilds. So without delay a photo was taken, passport forms completed and tickets booked to Perpignan. Everything was new. Sleeping in couchettes on the overnight train, driving through olive groves, vineyards, and finally arriving at the seaside town of Banyuls-sur-Mer, with its terracotta houses and soft blue shutters. Days were spent swimming in the sea, collecting shells and watching fishing boats unload their catch in the harbour. And when Victor's secretary Anne was free, she took us up mountain tracks to show us the Pyrenees Mountains and how close we were to Spain. And as we picnicked on baguettes filled with salami and French cheese, we saw farmers, faces weathered by the sun, load up their mules with fresh produce and wood for the winter.

'Shall we go to Spain?' Victor asked one morning at breakfast. On holiday he was more playful, always looking for an adventure.

'How long will it take?' asked Tess.

'We'll be there for lunch.'

The road was narrow, the surface rough and there were numerous potholes gouged out by the winter weather. Before long the incline got steeper, there was a succession of sharp hairpin bends and Victor did not hold back. As we were swung from one side of the car to the other, I craned my neck to see out of the window and caught sight of the sheer drop below. I shouted at Victor to slow down, which made him go faster, enjoying the screeches and squeals of laughter from the rear.

'And no petrol stations up here either,' he teased to intensify the drama.

Tess smiled, amused to see her husband play racing driver behind the wheel of the car. Finally the road levelled off and we came to a viewing point with a sign saying: '*España*'. It was the second foreign country I had been to within a week, so an occasion was made of stepping out onto Spanish soil. A little further on we found a mountain restaurant, with low wooden beams and an open fire and settled ourselves at a corner table.

'Spanish omelette?' Victor suggested.

'What's that?' I asked.

'An omelette with potatoes, onions, peppers... whatever is available,' Victor explained. 'You'll like it. In every country you'll find a staple meal that uses up the leftovers.'

'*Tortilla española y sangría para tres por favor,*' Victor ordered in Spanish.

I knew that he was fluent in French, but I did not know he could speak Spanish. Victor seemed to be at ease wherever he was.

Over time, I became more relaxed at the Rothschilds and feelings of homesickness abated. At least when I was at Merton Hall, I was away from my mother's moods. But there were tests of another kind. In Cambridge academic circles, the focus was always on scholarship and I knew that I could not compete. I preferred to remain in my imaginary world. But Victor was always on a quest to find out more about my capabilities, which he did more out of curiosity than judgment.

'Biff, why does a volcano erupt?'

I did not know the answer, nor felt like admitting it, so I left it to others to swallow up the question, which they did readily. Instead I leaned against the French window, pressed my nose against the glass and watched the shadows cast by the wisteria dance around the terrace. The sun bathed the garden with a warm evening glow and I noticed the croquet hoops set out on the lawn. I felt like going and hitting a ball. In the background I heard the conversation move on to different kinds of earth movements, the ability to forecast them and their effect on the population and environment.

'Biff,' Victor addressed me, bringing me out of my reverie. 'Can you look up the word *seismology*? The dictionary is over there.'

He pointed to a bookcase where there were ten volumes of the Oxford English Dictionary. I walked across the room slowly, staring at the carpet in search of inspiration. As I scanned the line of books I sang the alphabet inside my head, wishing I could remember the order of the 'r's, 's's and 't's. After a while I found the correct volume, knelt on the floor and opened the dictionary with apprehension. There were too many words and the type was so small. I turned the pages, unsure whether I should be going forward or back. The expectant silence in the room made it difficult to focus. The print blurred, my mind became more confused and all I could see was the grey-blue of the page as one letter merged into another.

'Well?' Victor asked.

I sensed discomfort among the guests.

'I-I...' I stuttered.

There was nothing to say as I could not find the word. But in that hesitation, suddenly the haze of confusion lifted. I realised that what he asked me to do was stupid. He was blind to it and I could see it, even though I was only eight years old. There was no point in making an example of me in front of his guests. It neither presented him in a good light nor taught me anything. I also doubted he gained satisfaction from watching me stumble. Suddenly the page came back into focus, I sorted out my alphabet, found the word and said its meaning indifferently. But in that instant, a spark ignited within me. I realised that being clever and being wise were completely different... and I wanted wisdom. I had no interest in the competitive world of academic achievement but wanted to understand how people think and feel.

Tess was gentler in the way she educated us, but sometimes she took us by surprise.

'Do you know who runs the world?' she asked, by way of confiding in us.

As neither Emma nor I had any idea, we waited for her to explain.

'It's the Freemasons,' she said matter-of-factly.

'Who are they?' asked Emma.

'No one really knows. It's a secret society.'

I remained silent, feeling out of my depth.

Tess continued: 'It's not easy to become one. You have to go through rigorous tests and procedures to be accepted. There are secret rituals and ceremonies which involve dressing up with swords and ropes and so on. But it's only for men. It takes years to climb up the ladder to become a Master Mason.'

'Why would you become one?' Emma enquired.

'Masons have power. They influence what happens in the world.'

'How?'

'They are everywhere – within government, business, banks and the military. But nobody knows exactly who they are. They have secret signs so they recognise one another.'

'Have you met any?' I asked.

Tess looked askance. 'Yes, there's one I know well.'

I presumed she was referring to Victor. I could imagine him being in a secret society that had designs on running the world.

However, I could not imagine him dressing up in strange clothes and taking part in rituals. But perhaps there were sides to Victor that I did not know?

'Have there always been secret societies?' I asked.

'Some say the Masons built Solomon's Temple. Yes, they have been around for thousands of years. It's just the names that change throughout the ages. The Knights Templar had one face for the public and another they kept secret. None of us know what goes on behind the seats of power.'

Tess was freer to express herself when Victor was not there. When he was present, her responsibility primarily was to answer to his needs. So when Victor wanted me to see a doctor in London, it was Tess who made the appointment. I was confused as there was nothing wrong with me, but I was assured that an occasion would be made of the trip. My mother and I were chauffeur-driven to the Rothschilds' flat in St James's Place and Tess accompanied us to the appointment with a promise of lunch afterwards. We were welcomed into a plush suite, which contrasted sharply to the drabness of our local doctor's waiting room. I was then shown into a consulting room, where I sat in a large armchair looking across a leather-topped desk at the doctor, who was smiling sympathetically. Then the questions began. Some I could not answer so my mother filled in the gaps. I was then weighed, measured and had blood samples taken, but the recurring thought in my mind was why I was there. I was fit and healthy after all. The only times I had been ill were when I had chickenpox and mumps. Apart from that, there had never been anything wrong with me.

It was a few days before the results came back. Everyone seemed reassured to know that I was well. However from snippets of conversations, I gathered that Victor had been concerned about my height. I knew that I was small for my age, but my mother kept assuring me that she had put on a spurt of growth in her teens and that there was nothing to worry about. But I was always compared with Emma. She was not only a head taller than me but had a well-defined bone structure and a slim figure, which gave her elegance and grace. I also envied her shoulder-length hair, as my mother kept mine cropped, which made me feel like a boy. Tess also bought Emma fashionable three quarter-length trousers and well-fitting jeans, while my clothes were hand-me-downs or bought too large so they would last. In truth, I felt like a frump beside Emma. So the next time I saw Victor, I asked him why he had sent me to the doctor.

'Your father is tall and you are small. I wondered why.'

And yes, my father was well over six foot, good-looking and known for his rugged features and gentle manner. I wished I was more like him.

A Lone Path

Time spent with my mother was usually for the benefit of our education. It seemed she did not know how to play. She left that to my brothers, who built Teresa and me a house in the walnut tree and made up games using the swing, trapeze and a rope that hung from it. But my mother was conscientious about reading to us, although the books she chose were far beyond my age so I could never follow the story. And while she read, my sister or I had to stroke her feet, a duty that I both resented and disliked, but she said it was the only way she could relax. Her other responsibilities entailed supervising piano practice and teaching us French from a book called *French without Tears*. These were the times I feared the most. With my mother glowering over my shoulder, my fingers trembled as I practised scales or tried a simple version of Pachelbel's Canon. If I made one too many errors, she would lose control and the shouting began, which invariably ended up in me running off to my room to escape. Learning French was worse. If I could not conjugate a verb, she would berate me until I broke down in tears and then spit out the words: 'Stop blubbing, Elizabeth.'

Only once did I stutter a response: 'B-but this is supposed to be without tears.'

My sister was more confident and outgoing than me and found it easier to deflect my mother's temper. She won praise effortlessly, while I always had to earn it. When my mother had a dinner party, I was the one who laid the table, arranged a posy of flowers as a centrepiece and ran errands for her in the kitchen while she prepared the meal. Then the following morning I made sure that I was first downstairs to do the previous night's washing-up before breakfast, which never failed to bring a smile to her face.

'My darling, you are an angel.'

And this was the kind of appreciation I craved.

But my mother's mood always changed when she took Teresa and me to London. She was proud to show us around the Natural History Museum, the Tower of London and Madame Tussauds, regaling us with stories about historical figures and watching our reactions of shock or amazement. But she was cautious about taking us to the Chamber of Horrors, as when I heard that the Princes in the Tower were suffocated while they were asleep, I had nightmares.

However, the highlight of our trips to London was visiting Bob at his flat in 1 Eaton Square. The sitting room, which doubled as his study, was comfortable and welcoming, and along the passageway were two bedrooms and a small dining room where Gordon, his manservant, put up camp beds for Teresa and me when we stayed the night. Bob was invariably in his pyjamas when we arrived, but his clothes were laid out ready for him on the bed. And when he did get dressed, he looked dashing in a tweed suit, waistcoat, bow tie and a watch chain to give a final flourish. I always felt at home in Bob's flat. It was not just the presents he gave us but his fun-loving nature and openness that allowed us to say what we wanted and also be heard. He told us tales about his adventures on the gambling tables, amounts he had won and lost, and why he was never content to pocket his winnings and leave.

'It's the element of risk that gives the thrill. The adrenaline rush when the cards are dealt, the turntable spun, knowing that a possible fortune lies in one throw. If not that time, it'll be the next.'

And I understood why he was always drawn to another game, another bet, even if he blew all his winnings in the process.

I could talk to Bob about anything. The word 'sex' was written on a handout that I was given in a fortune telling, and when I asked my mother what it meant, she avoided the question.

'Ask Bob,' she smiled.

So I did.

'There are two sexes – one male and one female – the boys and the girls.'

From my mother's response, I guessed there was more to it, but that was the only sex education I ever received.

My mother was different when she was with Bob. She became childlike, questioning, laughing at incidental jokes, which became more exaggerated when Bob teased her. Across the dining table, I noticed her flush when he asked about her recent lunch with Jim Geraghty, the art editor of the *New Yorker* magazine.

'Is he your new paramour?' Bob asked, unabashed.

My mother looked away before answering: 'We had lunch together, that's all. Jim offered me some prints of the magazine's best cartoons and wanted me to choose some. I love them.'

'…or is it Jim that you love?' Bob queried mischievously.

The atmosphere changed when my father was there. As he worked in London during the week, he made the occasional appearance when we were at Bob's flat. As was customary, conversation reverted to his favourite opera singers and arias as Bob and my father were both regular attendants at Covent Garden Opera House.

'I've bought tickets in the stalls for you to see Meistersinger,' Bob said, knowing how much this would please my father.

My father was visibly touched by this act of generosity as he only sat 'in the gods' where the seats were cheapest. Bob cared for my father in other ways too. They both suffered from bad backs and Bob swore by an osteopath called Stephen Ward. Once the introduction had been made, my father booked an appointment and from thereon became an enthusiastic advocate of his skills.

'He's not only managed to get rid of my back pain but also has great charm. I like him enormously.'

Yet for some reason it felt strange having my father sitting at one end of the dining table and Bob at the other. There was a formality about the occasion that was not there when it was just Bob, my mother, Teresa and me. So at times like these, I focussed on my food. Gordon knew my favourite meal was lamb cutlets and crisp roast potatoes, followed by ice cream and fruit for dessert. But Bob always finished his meal with a digestive biscuit and cheddar cheese topped off with a bit of English mustard.

'How can you eat mustard with cheese?' I asked with a grimace.

'It's a natural combination of tastes. Try some.'

He gave me half his biscuit and to my surprise I enjoyed it.

'You see, it's important to try new things, otherwise you don't know what you're missing.'

After that, he introduced me to roast pheasant, smoked salmon and caviar, which caused some concern for my parents as I loved the taste of them all.

Bob liked to surprise us too. One summer he rented a house in Littlehampton for our family to have a holiday, although my father said he would prefer to join us afterwards in Cornwall. I was curious to see a different seascape with stretches of sand instead of cliffs and coves. The house was grander than I expected, with numerous bedrooms, two large sitting rooms and a garden that led down to the beach. Swimming, croquet matches, rambling walks and meals cooked by Gordon gave my mother a break and offered us a sense of luxury that I had not experienced before.

One afternoon, my mother took Teresa and me for a walk along the coastal path. The scent of freshly mown grass wafted around us. As we approached a gate my sister ran ahead to open it, but I wanted to climb it. I did not see that it was already ajar and as I put my leg over the top rung, Teresa pushed the gate shut and I fell. I was not sure whether it was the sight of the blood flowing down my face or the pain that shot through my shoulder that made me cry out.

'Help me get her up,' my mother urged my sister, reassuring her that it was not her fault.

'It's my arm,' I whimpered.

'Keep it still. We'll have to take you to hospital.'

X-rays and examinations confirmed a broken collarbone and a deep cut on my head.

'It'll mend quickly,' the doctor assured me, 'but I'm afraid you'll have to wear a sling, which means no swimming for a month.'

It was hot weather and I dreaded the thought of not being able to go into the sea. But what alarmed me more was seeing the nurse get out a needle and thread to sew up my head. I screamed.

She laughed: 'It's to stitch up the sling, not your head.'

That evening, Bob asked me to sit beside him and he put his arm around me.

'What a brave little girl you are. I'm going to give you a present.'

'What?' I asked, expecting a bar of chocolate.

'It's up to you,' he said. 'You can have anything you want.'

'I don't understand,' I replied, puzzled by his response.

'You can have anything in the world you want,' Bob confirmed. 'The choice is yours.'

I looked at Joan questioningly.

'Well,' she said, 'that's something for you to think about tonight.'

'Anything?' I said, looking at Bob again.

'Yes, anything.'

And that was the side of Bob that I loved the most. How could anyone be rash enough to offer such a gift to a young girl and have the courage to carry it out? But I knew he was a risk taker. I spent the evening in a daze as different ideas tumbled around my mind. I had always wanted a doll but had never been allowed one, but I was too old for that now. Nevertheless I wanted something I could hold, care for, and the idea of a furry animal, a pet, came to mind. I knew my father disliked cats as they messed in the garden, but maybe I would be allowed a puppy?

'What do you think, Joan?'

I could see from her expression that she thought it unlikely.

'Try something else. What do you enjoy doing?' she asked.

I loved watching people and was often told off for staring. I was fascinated by expressions, mannerisms and remembered the weathered faces of the farmers and fishermen in France. I was no painter, but I maybe I could capture them on film?

'How about a camera?'

'Ask Bob. You can start by taking a picture of me.' Joan smiled.

The following morning, I asked Bob if he had meant what he said.

'I don't break promises,' he reassured me. 'Have you thought?'

'Yes.'

'And?'

'A puppy or a camera.'

'Then a camera you shall have. Let's go and buy one now.'

And off we went. There were no conditions or hesitations... just unbridled generosity. By the end of the day, I had a Brownie Box camera, two reels of film and, despite the encumbrance of having my arm in a sling, I had managed to take my first photographs. But it was not long before the camera was set to one side as another change was afoot.

My mother had warned that either my sister or I would have to go to boarding school as one of us at home was enough. When she asked who it was to be and I saw Teresa's lip tremble, I felt compassion for her and offered to go myself, imagining it would not be for a while. Only then did my mother break the news that

Merton Hall School was closing as Emma was going to Cranbourne Chase Boarding School.

'So what will happen to the rest of us?' I asked.

'The other children will return to primary school, but we thought you could go directly to boarding school. We've arranged to see Badminton in Bristol. It's a progressive school with an excellent headmistress.'

The reality of spending most of the year alone on the other side of the country filled me with dread. Any chance of finding the love and security that I so desperately craved was rapidly disappearing. I would not even have Joan or my sister for support. But I guessed that Joan would not be with us much longer as she had met a sailor and was talking about getting married. Nevertheless, it came as a shock when she broke the news.

'I'll be leaving soon,' she confided. 'But you'll be away at school so you won't miss me.'

'I will,' I said with a lump in my throat. 'Are you going to marry the sailor?'

'Yes, so I'll be moving away too.'

I was pleased for her but dismayed that her boyfriend had come before me.

'I'll come and see you, though,' she said reassuringly.

'Not if I'm in Bristol.'

She took me in her arms. 'You'll be alright, Elizabeth. You may be happier if you're away from home.'

'I won't be.'

And glimpsing tears in her eyes, I imagined that she was not only concerned about my future, but her own too.

I had just had my tenth birthday when, on a dismal January day, my mother drove me to Bristol to begin my first term at boarding school. It was dark when we turned into the driveway of the junior school. As we walked up the steps to the main entrance, I could feel myself shivering. It felt like walking into a prison. We were greeted formally by the matron, who confirmed that my trunk had arrived, so my mother put her hand on my shoulder and said, 'Right, I'll be off now. I'll write to you once a week.'

And with a peck on my cheek, she drove away.

For the most part I allowed the tears to flow in private, either in the bathroom or under the bedclothes at night. But it was not long before my emotional pain expressed itself physically and I began suffering from excruciating earache. The matron was both severe in manner and appearance. No hot water bottle or aspirin was offered, nor was there sympathy or advice. It was a Jewish girl called Judith, who seemed to understand. She talked to me gently, gave me tips on how to cope with the rules and routine, and told me stories about the other children. Gradually I got my bearings and found ways of relating to some of the other girls in my class. It was weekends and half terms that I found most difficult. As most of the children lived within an hour's drive of Bristol, their parents came to take them out and they returned with homemade cakes, scones and sweets. It was then that I realised that my parents would never visit me, nor would I ever have a tuck box.

The school must have told my parents that I had difficulty settling in as when it came to my second term, Bob offered to accompany my mother and me. He confided that he had been sent to boarding school a long way from home and had pleaded with his parents to rescue him, so he understood how I felt and sympathised. He booked us rooms in a Bristol hotel, so we could stay the night before term began to make the transition easier. But the formality of hotel meals, starched serviettes and too many knives and forks to choose from made me feel uncomfortable.

While Bob and my mother relaxed in each other's company, I felt as though I was marking time, waiting for my sentence to begin. As it turned out, Bob chose not to come with us to the school. Maybe he did not want to relive the emotion he had experienced all those years ago, or perhaps it would have been strange having him there instead of my father? Once again, my mother's farewell was perfunctory, but as a sop she added that Tess was planning on taking Emma and me skiing during the winter holidays. I had imagined our lives would take separate paths from now on, so the thought of skiing in the Alps served as an incentive to get through the term.

When the holidays came, I was told we were going to the Swiss resort of Wengen as Victor's sister Miriam, a well-respected scientist like her brother, took her children there each year. But as they were proficient skiers and Emma and I were beginners, we had our own ski instructor in the mornings and skating lessons in the afternoon. There were the usual grumbles after breakfast as we put on scratchy ski socks and laced up uncomfortable boots, but once we got on the slopes, all was forgotten and we challenged each other to go faster, negotiate more difficult terrain, even trying small jumps.

As our confidence grew, our guide took us higher – by train up to Scheidegg just below the Jungfrau; and from there he would guide us back to the village through forest trails on a tour that I wished would never end. At the end of the day, we met Miriam's children for hot chocolate before returning to the hotel for broths thickened with vermicelli or *käse fondue*, before collapsing into bed under sumptuous, weightless duvets. We returned to Wengen the following two years and, as our skiing improved, Emma and I progressed to more challenging runs. But on a day when it was snowing hard and visibility was poor, I hit a mogul field, lost control and fell awkwardly. A horse-drawn sled took me off the mountain and an X-ray confirmed a torn cruciate ligament, and after that I never went skiing with the Rothschilds again.

Instead it was Barbados for Christmas. Although I was excited by the idea of seeing a tropical island, I was nervous about being away from home for two consecutive terms as well as the intervening holiday. Once again my mother persuaded me that it was a lifetime opportunity and not to be missed. It was my first time in an aeroplane, a long-haul flight with a refuelling stop in Newfoundland. But we travelled first class, Emma and I had pull-down beds, so we slept and the journey went quickly. When we arrived at the prestigious Sandy Lane resort, the house where we were staying reminded me of a Greek temple with a central hall framed by pillars and east and west wings that gave access to the bedrooms. The terrace, shaded by palm trees, led directly onto the beach.

Instead of snow-skiing, Emma and I spent the mornings skiing on water. We learned to pull ourselves upright, follow in the wake of the boat and, when our time was up, sink gracefully into the water and wait to be picked up by the boat. Once again, having a personal instructor enabled us to progress quickly and it was not long before we were able to balance on one ski, slalom either side of the wake and be towed as a twosome. There was a sense of exhilaration going fast over water and seeing the coastline fleeting by. After a fresh limeade and lunch, we snorkelled from the shore, gazing in wonder at the multi-coloured reef fish, corals and shells that neither of us had ever seen before.

In the evenings Emma and I took on Victor at table tennis. He showed us how to hold the bat Chinese style, and if I aimed well and hit hard he could not return my shots, bringing a smile to my face and surprise to his. Tess joined us for cards to make up a foursome, but playing with the three of them, I doubted I would ever win. I reminded myself it was only a game and took on the challenge of distracting my opponents in the hope they would make a mistake. I knew that Victor never missed my tricks but for the most part chose to ignore them. Occasionally though, he would pounce back, showing that nothing got passed him. So I devised increasingly ingenious ways to fool him, acting out ridiculous scenarios so I could lean on his shoulder and peek at his cards. In this way cheating became more fun than the game itself and we spent the evenings in laughter.

I returned to England feeling more grown up and prettier. Tess had arranged for me to have my hair cut by a French stylist, bought me some new clothes and my skin was browned by the sun. When I returned to school, a new girl asked if I was from India and I enjoyed the idea of being a foreigner. But that was the last holiday I spent with the Rothschilds. From then on it was deemed best for Emma and I to be kept apart owing to the significant discrepancy between her intellectual ability and mine. It was thirty years before I saw her again.

RETURN TO CAMBRIDGE

～

The decision to separate Emma and me was validated three years later when I was relegated to the B stream at thirteen years old. I had been diligent with my studies, achieved top results, so there was genuine surprise amongst my classmates.

'Doesn't make sense. You got an honours' average.'

I escaped to my dormitory to hide my tears. I had now been formally labelled second-rate. My housemistress came to console me.

'You mustn't take this personally, Biff. We thought it was best for you to be top of the B group, rather than bottom of the A group.'

My nickname had stuck and seemed relevant in the present circumstances. But this time, instead of being judged by my mother, it was by a panel of teachers.

I found solace in English lessons. Reading plays, poetry, prose and writing gave me a chance to explore deeper feelings. When I was asked to write an essay on loneliness, I was familiar with the subject matter.

'To be alone and to be lonely are two quite different things…'

My teacher commended me as I was only person who had made the distinction. She went on to praise my insights on character, plot and storylines in English literature, and encouraged me to join the school drama group. This aroused interest from my father. He had studied Classics in Cambridge, then switched to English and ever since the theatre had always been an important part in his life. When I told him I had been chosen to play the lead in Christopher Fry's *The Boy and the Cart*, he said he would like to see it. Whether it was a belated sense of duty or a genuine interest in seeing me act I was unsure, but I was pleased he wanted to come as he had never been to the school. His comments about plays and playwrights attracted the attention of the teachers, and I was proud to see him mingling with staff, sharing his knowledge. And when our play won the competition, he gave me an affectionate pat on my shoulder and said quietly, 'Well done.'

With a flush of pride, I replied, 'I'm glad you came.'

But in that brief exchange, I realised how much had been left unsaid. I wanted to tell him how much his presence had meant to me, that I now had a memory of school that I would always treasure, but expressing the truth of my feelings in this way would have felt awkward and inappropriate. Yet had I done so, the invisible barrier between us may have melted away and opened up a pathway of communication.

Being relegated to the B stream made me want to leave school as soon as I was old enough. But when I told my mother, I received a harsh rebuke.

'How dare you throw away the chances we've given you by sending you to boarding school? Anyway, you need more exams before you leave.'

I had passed English Literature, Latin and Biology, but failed two crucial exams, Maths and English Language. As these subjects were deemed vital to secure a place at any college or institution, there was concern about what I was going to do. So I agreed to stay on and retake English, but when I failed the subject once again my parents changed their mind. As my mother marked English O-level papers and my father English A-level, they conceded that I might do better spending a year at home, where they would be able to give me some help.

I left school on St Patrick's Day with a gift of shamrock from my friends. I was just sixteen at the time. I returned to Cambridge with a renewed sense of hope that life at home might now be different. My brothers had left – Nic to be an archaeologist and Sebastian a doctor – and my sister had gone to secretarial college in London. My father was now working at the Cambridge branch of the University Press, so for the first time I would have the undivided attention of my parents. As I sat on the garden terrace looking across the fringe of pink roses that edged the lawn, I was lulled by a sense of peace. It felt as though I had come home at last.

The first change I made was not to answer to the name of Biff anymore. Instead I asked to be called Eliza. It was time to move on from childhood. Then within the social circle of my parents' friends, I began exploring ideas as to what line of work I could do. It was Dadie Rylands who came up with an idea. He was a Fellow of King's College, had taught my father English at university and now commanded respect from professors, students and authors as a doyen of English literature. His fascination with people and what motivated them prompted him to take an interest in me.

'How about helping out at the Arts Theatre?' he suggested.

'In what capacity?' I asked. 'I have no training.'

'Theatre is a microcosm of life. All kinds of skills are needed – costumes, props, sets, lighting, stage management. As a patron, I could ask on your behalf.'

Dadie had a knack of making those around him feel at ease, whatever their age or ability. He was not only a frequent visitor at home, but every summer came on holiday with us in Cornwall. Whether it was conversations about the best way to wash up or characters in a Hardy novel, he was always able to inspire those around him with his wit and good humour. Without delay, he made enquiries, and soon I heard that the head of the wardrobe department had said she would be glad of some help. Judy was large in stature and generous by nature. As I pushed my way through the rails of costumes to her sewing table, she greeted me with a broad smile.

'Welcome, Eliza. We keep things simple here. We use two colours of thread for everything – black and white. You don't need to be a seamstress here, just to have an eye for what looks right. We do as much dressing down as dressing up... making outfits that look natural and authentic. From what Dadie said about you, I think you'll like it.'

She was right. I enjoyed being creative in the world of make-believe, finding ingenious ways to bridge the gap between illusion and reality.

But soon I was to find out that the dividing line between the two was not confined to the theatre. It concerned an incident involving Bob, which prompted me to question whether he was telling the truth or not. I had always regarded him as a maverick, which maybe was one of the reasons I found it easy to relax in his company. His ability to charm and challenge without minding what others might think, made a refreshing change from my parents' friends who were more inclined to follow etiquette and convention. So when I heard that Bob was in trouble and had asked to come and stay, I was intrigued.

He arrived with the customary bottle of whisky and promptly poured himself a glass, even though it was mid-afternoon. He appeared shaken, although there was a bullish tone when he spoke. He told us that someone of questionable reputation called Ronnie Kray had approached him about a possible business deal in Nigeria. Bob had met him on three occasions and chosen to decline his offer. But recently, headlines in the *Sunday Mirror* had alluded to a friendship between a peer and a gangster, so questions were now being asked. Bob explained that he had been on holiday in Vittel with his friend Colin Coote when the story broke and they had joked about who the peer might be. It was only when he got home that a fellow member of Parliament, Tom Driberg, revealed that the peer was him. I noticed a look of concern on my mother's face.

Bob continued: 'After the Profumo affair last year, the Government can't afford another scandal so they want to kill the story as quickly as possible. Owing to this, I'm being offered the best legal advice.'

'Who from?' asked my mother.

'Arnold Goodman, who's recommending Gerald Gardiner as my QC. I trust them both implicitly. Under Gardiner's supervision, I've written a stinker of a letter to *The Times* admitting that I'm the peer in question but refuting the allegations that are being made. I explain the circumstances in which I met Ronnie Kray and warn about the grave danger to public life when the press jump to conclusions without being in possession of the full facts. Bringing the story into the open will floor the *Sunday Mirror* and they'll be left with egg on their face, you'll see. Goodman believes they'll offer me a handsome compensation to bring the matter to a close quickly.'

Bob helped himself to another whisky before continuing.

'The letter's going to be published tomorrow. That's why I had to leave London. I've been advised not to talk to anyone until the whole thing blows over… it's such a relief to be here.'

As I listened, I wondered about the authenticity of Bob's story. On a recent visit to Eaton Square, I had met someone called Ronnie Kray, who seemed an unlikely friend of Bob's. He had greased-down hair, an East End accent and to me seemed sleazy. I felt uneasy in his company and wondered what he was doing in Bob's flat. Bob chose to introduce me as his goddaughter, we shook hands and shortly afterwards he left. I remembered another incident too, when I was driving to London with my sister. Suddenly she experienced pain and swelling in her hands and we were alarmed as to what it could be. We went straight to Bob's flat and he called the doctor, who diagnosed rheumatic fever and advised her to stay in bed. While she was unwell, Bob and Gordon took care of her but, during her stay, Ronnie Kray paid a visit and gave her a large bouquet of red roses. If this were the man in question, the relationship between him and Bob certainly appeared to be more than a potential business partnership.

When my father arrived home, Bob had gone for a rest, which gave my mother a chance to explain why he had come. Concerned about the unexpected intrusion, my father asked how long he would be staying.

'Presumably until the story dies down.'

'But that could be a while,' my father replied, clearly irritated.

Whether it was the whisky, wine or Bob's more buoyant mood, the atmosphere relaxed during the evening. He reassured my parents that the story would be an overnight affair and that the *Sunday Mirror* would soon be grovelling and offering payment for the damage caused.

'I trust Gerald Gardener completely,' Bob insisted again. 'When you look into those piercing, steel-grey eyes, you know he'll not stand for any nonsense. All he wants is to expose the lies. I have total confidence in him.'

The following morning Bob proudly showed us his letter to *The Times* before devouring the commentary in the rest of the papers. Then the phone began to ring. When he heard that James Margach, the political correspondent of the *Sunday Times,* had tracked him down, Bob was tempted to offer him an interview.

'I know Margach. He's an honest journalist.'

'Can you trust anyone at the moment?' my mother asked, knowing that he had been asked to maintain a low profile.

'I've had dealings with James in the past and he's a good man. I've no intention of talking to anybody else, but this is a chance to tell my side of the story.'

Whether Bob had permission or not, it was clear that he had made up his mind to grant him an interview. Within the hour, Margach had been invited to the house on condition that the meeting would be kept secret. When he arrived, my mother disappeared to avoid being seen, so I showed him into the drawing room. The journalist seemed genial and friendly and I judged Bob's assessment of him was probably right. I noticed him taking in his surroundings, presumably wondering why Bob had chosen our house as his hideaway, before suggesting they go into the garden to do the interview. When he had finished, I saw him out and noticed a couple of other journalists at the gate. It seemed that word had got out about Bob's whereabouts.

When my father returned from work, several more reporters had joined them, making it difficult for him to get into the house. He did not hide his temper. With Bob out of the room, he spat out the words: 'This is intolerable. I've had enough. Bob has to leave.'

I was taken aback at seeing my father so angry and noticed my mother's discomfort. She had offered Bob sanctuary at a time of need but could not ignore the feelings of her husband, who valued his privacy above all else. Her loyalties were clearly divided.

'I'll ask him to go first thing in the morning,' she assured my father and then turned to me. 'Can you get rid of the journalists?'

'How?'

'Just tell them to go away. Say Bob has no intention of talking to them.'

'They won't believe me.'

I was surprised that her instruction did not bother me. In the four months I had been at home, my confidence had grown. I had bought new clothes and a pair of suede lace-up boots and no longer felt like an awkward schoolgirl. So, with a smile on my face, I approached the journalists.

'Bob has no intention of giving any more interviews.'

They asked who I was, how I knew Bob and why he was staying at our house.

'Never you mind,' I said. 'Why not go to the pub instead of wasting your time here? That's where Bob was last night.'

And it was true. There was a pub a short distance from our house, where Bob had been the previous evening winning the support of the locals. Realising there was little more I could do to get rid of them, I went inside to read the Margach article. As I suspected, there was a detailed description of our house, making it out to be far grander than it was, with exaggerated descriptions of ornaments, furnishings and its sense of seclusion. I smiled to myself. We lived on a busy road, it was a comfortable house, but certainly not grand, nor a hideaway. So what with Margach's comments about our home and Bob's portrayal of his relationship with Ronnie Kray, I wondered whether I could trust anything that was written in the press.

It was not long before we heard that Bob had won a resounding victory, culminating in him being paid compensation by the Mirror group of forty thousand pounds. Apparently it was unheard of for such a large amount of money to be paid voluntarily by a newspaper group. But as Bob had explained, Arnold Goodman was neither going to allow the case to be trawled through the courts nor let the government be tainted by a story that he believed had no substance. Later my mother told me that Bob wanted to pass on some of the money to Teresa and me.

'He regards it as ill-gotten gains so wants to give most of it away. He's setting up some trust funds for close relations and you are to be one of the beneficiaries.'

'But he's always short of money himself,' I said with surprise.

'I know. But he feels uncomfortable about keeping this money. He wants to give Teresa fifteen thousand pounds as she is his goddaughter, and you ten. It will be held in trust until you're both twenty-five. You're both very fortunate. It's an amount of money that will set you up for life.'

I had difficulty in assimilating the news as I had no idea what such a large amount of money meant. But I was intrigued that Bob regarded the money as 'ill-gotten gains' and suspected that he may not have been entirely honest with either his legal team or the press.

Since being at secretarial college in London, Teresa had seen more of Bob. She lived with a friend in a flat in Chelsea so I presumed that Bob was helping her financially. During her school years, he had given her a covenant, bought her a car when she was seventeen and taken her on numerous trips abroad. I knew how much he loved her and through her teenage years had likened her to Gigi, the heroine of a 1958 film, a rebellious young girl who grew up to be a beautiful woman. Bob treated Teresa differently from his other godchildren and sometimes I wondered why. Then one day she confided that Bob had told her that he was her true father and she was his daughter. I was taken aback and asked Teresa if she thought it was true.

'No,' she replied confidently. 'If he was my father, why are you and I so alike?'

Certainly our voices were similar. We could easily fool people on the telephone and over the years had fun doing so. But Teresa had Bob's sociable, outgoing nature, while I was more introspective and quieter. He certainly treated her more like a daughter than a goddaughter. Also Teresa had been conceived during the war, when my father was away for long spells at sea. Initially, my mother had taken my brothers to Cornwall for safety, but she got bored and said that she would rather be bombed than spend any more time in such a remote place. So she had returned to Cambridge, where Bob had a post with the RAF. In the circumstances, it was not difficult to imagine that they had an affair.

Whatever the truth, I was touched that my sister had shared her secret. I also understood why she preferred to see herself as my father's daughter. Even though he found it difficult to relate to his children, he was sensitive, gentle and kind, as I discovered when he took me to the opera at Covent Garden.

'The secret of Wagner is to let it wash over you,' he explained over a sandwich and glass of wine at the Garrick Club before the opera began. He was taking me to *Tristan and Isolde,* but wanted to tell me the story first. As he did, I saw that for him life was mirrored in the great Wagnerian themes – heroism and sacrifice, love and death, illusion and fantasy. From the moment the curtain went up, he was visibly moved by the power, pace and magnificence of the music, and when the arias were sung, tears flowed down his cheeks. For him, music was a love potion, and as we watched the drama unfold, my heart went out to him and I felt close to him for the first time in my life.

But I also saw my father as a man weighed down by responsibility that was beginning to take its toll. As soon as he got back from work, he poured himself a gin and mixed and told my mother the latest challenge he was facing with the syndics of the University Press. He always found it difficult to reach a compromise with this panel of academics with entrenched views, who made the final decision on what books the press should publish. And my father disliked conflict.

'We need new blood,' my father would say, 'someone who can stand up to them.'

My father was a progressive who realised that the University Press was in danger of becoming fossilised unless he could find a successor to move things on. I listened to his concerns and did my best to understand the complexities of the academic and business world and offered my sympathy where I could.

But in reaching out to him, I wanted him to do the same for me – to find out who I was and the person I was becoming. Yet no matter what I did, the door remained closed. So gradually I began to accept that we were walking different paths and there was nothing I could do to change this. It seemed I had a father who was absent from my life and indifferent to my feelings.

HERSCHEL ROAD

~

Victor had leased Merton Hall from St John's College in the early thirties but, as with Ashton House, the university now wanted the historic building back. So the Rothschilds bought some land on the outskirts of Cambridge close to the countryside and asked their friend Richard Llewellyn Davies to design a house for them. By the time I left school, the Rothschilds had moved into their new home in Herschel Road. It had a similar layout to Merton Hall, with a large drawing room adjoining Victor's study on one side and the dining room on the other. Floor-to-ceiling glass spanned the length of each downstairs room and sliding doors opened onto lawns, rose gardens, a tennis court and a pathway that led to a covered swimming pool. The sumptuous sofas and armchairs gave a sense of luxury, yet the soft neutral colours and uncluttered walls made the house feel unpretentious. A Cezanne painting hung in pride of place above the fireplace.

Since being away at boarding school, I had kept in touch with Victor and Tess, but Emma and I had deliberately been kept apart... a prescient decision as at the age of fifteen, Emma had won a major scholarship to Oxford, the youngest student ever to achieve such an accolade. The Rothschilds had a wide circle of friends – eminent scientists, philosophers, economists, writers and artists

– but there was group of eight who met regularly. These included my godfather Alan Hodgkin, a research scientist and Nobel Prize winner and his wife Marni; Noel Annan, Provost of King's College and his German-born wife Gabriele; and my parents. Apart from Gabriele and Marni, they had all been close friends since university days with Tess and my mother meeting during their first year at Newnham College.

Since then they had all taken an interest in seeking political solutions for the problems of the world and times together were spent in avid discussion on how this could best be done. At university, Victor, Noel and Alan had been members of a private debating society, the Apostles, which espoused left-wing ideas and communist ideals. Other members included Guy Burgess, Donald Maclean and Kim Philby, who came together to form the Cambridge spy ring. My mother described Guy as being good company, fun-loving, easy to be around and how difficult she found it to believe the scale of his betrayal. Indeed, as one spy was outed and then another, this close-knit group of friends was left in disbelief. But I recognised how easy it is to be deceived as we never know what goes on in another's mind.

Visits to Herschel Road always followed the same routine – a swim in the heated pool followed by drinks in the drawing room. Tess greeted us, gracious and elegant as ever, her facial features softening with age and now framed by silvery grey hair. Victor always sat in the same chair, with a table near at hand for his drink and an ashtray as he was rarely without a Sobranie cigarette. He dressed casually in grey flannel trousers and a white open-necked shirt as he had a dislike of formal wear. And whoever was there, Victor was always on a mission to probe, ask questions and unearth information to which otherwise he would not have been privy. But when I was present, whatever impassioned conversation was taking place, Victor's voice boomed across the room.

'Biff, come and sit next to me.'

I could have felt bidden, but there was no hint of that in his manner. On the contrary, I felt privileged. As I sat on the sofa beside him, he would turn his attention away from the other guests to engage me in conversation. He asked how I was faring, whether my mother was behaving herself, what food she was giving me and what I was going to do with my life. I always felt relaxed in his company, touched that someone of his calibre was taking a personal interest in me.

There were times, however, when he surprised me.

'Is your passport in date?' he asked out of the blue.

'I think so.'

'I want you to go to Paris for the day and bring back some foie gras for a dinner party.'

'That's ridiculous.' I laughed. 'You can buy foie gras here.'

'But I want it bought in Paris,' he insisted. 'You can collect it from Miranda's flat.'

Miranda was his youngest daughter by his ex-wife Barbara. I remembered her being beautiful and vivacious with shoulder-length auburn hair. But the thought of driving to Heathrow, catching flights and finding her flat felt daunting, especially as I had only just passed my driving test. However, Victor was quick to reassure me that Anne would book my flights, give me money for taxis and that the drive to Heathrow Airport was not difficult.

'It will do you good,' he smiled, assuming that I had already agreed.

My mother had taught me to drive and surprisingly had shown patience and understanding as I learned to reverse and do three-point turns. When I passed my test, she then encouraged me to buy a second-hand car with money that Tess had given me. I imagined that she did not want me to feel outdone by Bob's gift of a car to Teresa shortly after her seventeenth birthday.

Before I went I asked my mother about Miranda.

'She married a Palestinian,' my mother explained, 'but sadly he died last year. They had only been together for a couple of years and she's now left with a daughter called Da'ad.'

'What happened?' I asked.

'He drowned… in shallow water.'

'How?' I asked, looking questioningly at her.

'I'm not sure. It all seems very strange.'

My mother went on to explain that Miranda was an idealist and imagined that if a Rothschild married a Moslem, it might help ease the Israeli-Palestinian conflict.

'So was he got rid of?'

My mother paused before saying, 'Well, yes… maybe.'

The story added a sense of mystery to my Paris adventure. I was curious to see Miranda again.

The alarm went off at four in the morning, but when I looked out a thick mist enveloped the garden. I felt apprehensive as I had never driven in poor visibility before. Tentatively I drove out of Cambridge, remembering to dip my lights, but the journey was slow as I could only see a short distance ahead. Before long, however, I had a car to follow and as I neared London, the mist lifted. Parking and finding my flight was no problem and it was with relief that I boarded the plane. As planned, I took a taxi to Miranda's flat, and as soon as I rang the bell, the door opened and I was welcomed with a warm embrace. As Miranda showed me around, she explained that the flat used to be a milliner's shop, hence the unusually large rooms. It felt unconventional, bohemian, and her artistic flair had brought colour and style to her home. A couple of friends were sitting at the dining table speaking French but broke off their conversation when they saw me to offer me a glass of wine.

'*Merci*,' I replied and then added, '*je ne peux pas parler Francais.*'

'But your accent is good,' one of them said in broken English. 'You speak as though you are French.'

I was glad of the compliment and put it down to having done a couple of French exchanges in the Dordogne in my early teens.

Lunch consisted of local cheeses, salami and salads accompanied by a warm baguette, which was welcome after my early start. The conversation soon got around to Victor and what I knew about the dinner party he was giving that night. I said that I was just the errand girl and had no idea why the occasion warranted foie gras from Paris.

Miranda laughed. 'He's crazy. He could have bought it from Fortnum and Mason.'

And she disappeared to collect the package but returned with two, both wrapped in brown paper and a similar size.

'I didn't know there was a second package,' I said, surprised.

Miranda raised her eyebrows and threw up her arms. 'None of us know what my father is up to.'

On the aeroplane, I asked the air steward to put the foie gras in the fridge and kept the other package with me. I wanted to accomplish my task to the best of my ability. Back on British soil, I enjoyed my drive back to Herschel Road, where I proudly presented Victor with the two packages.

'Did you enjoy your day?' he asked.

'I did.'

'And how was Miranda?'

'She was well. I liked her flat. She had some friends for lunch so I practised my French.'

I could see no sign of dinner preparations, so I asked if the foie gras was for tonight.

'It is.'

'Then I hope it's appreciated.'

I never said anything about the second package. I did not want to pry, aware that there was always an element of mystery around Victor. As I made a move to leave, he put his hand on my shoulder and drew me back.

'If you ever you need work, I'll take you on as my private secretary.'

'Oh yes,' I mocked, 'and what would I do?'

'We can decide later whether you taste wine or scrub floors.'

I laughed and wondered what my day had really been about. I guessed that the dinner party was a ruse and there was another reason for my trip to Paris.

Despite Victor's offer of work, the question remained as to what I was going to do. But when my mother told me that she had secured me a place at Atholl Crescent, a prestigious cookery school in Edinburgh, my heart sank. She had always said that I was 'good with my hands', which I took to be a euphemism for lacking intelligence so regarded it as a put-down. However, I never dreamed she would follow this through by sending me to domestic science college. She justified her decision by saying that if I became a high-class cook, I would be able to earn a good income by catering for exclusive dinner parties.

'But I don't want to cook,' I interrupted.

Ignoring my comment, she went on to say that the daughter of a friend had completed the course and was doing very well by offering this service in London.

'The course will stand you in good stead for the rest of your life,' my mother insisted. 'We've paid for your first term.'

She told me of the idea when my father was away so I could not appeal to him, although he always backed her up anyway. The last thing I wanted was to be sent away again to the other end of the country to learn Cordon Bleu cookery. All I needed was a kitchen to learn to cook. But if the daughters of the academic elite were not Oxbridge material, it seemed they were either destined to become secretaries or caterers… and I wanted to be neither.

Not long after this exchange, Victor invited me into his study. I liked the intimacy of his room with his books and papers spread about, black and white photographs of Tess and the children, and an assortment of gadgets to amuse himself. He drew up two chairs opposite one another and went straight to the point.

'Do you want to go to cookery school?'

'No,' I replied with conviction.

'So what are you going to do?'

'I don't know.'

'Saying "no" works best if you have an alternative plan.'

I tilted my head on one side, wondering what else I could do. It was true – if I had another idea, maybe my parents would listen.

'I like the theatre, what I'm doing now… working behind the scenes.'

'Is there a training in that?'

'I'm not sure.'

'Then find out,' Victor said at once. 'And when you come up with a viable alternative, let me know.'

'But they've paid for my first term. They won't want to lose that money.'

'Why not?' Victor asked. 'They made the decision without consulting you.'

Victor had a knack of pinpointing the problem and then finding a solution. I valued his directness, minimal use of words, no frills or flattery. His brevity brought clarity, so when I left I felt hopeful. If I came up with another idea, maybe my parents would listen. And if not, Victor would ensure that they did.

I began making enquiries and discovered a two-year stage-management course that was being offered at the Central School of Speech and Drama. I sent off application forms, was invited for an interview and told my parents of my plan. To my surprise, they expressed interest, wanted to know about the course and, as Victor had predicted, they did not object. The next time I saw him, I told him of my success but he neither wanted nor expected gratitude. His pleasure came from knowing that he had helped me make a U-turn that had paved a way for my future.

Before I left, I told him that I was now working for the Cambridge Footlights and had a met a couple of jazz enthusiasts.

Victor was a proficient jazz pianist himself, who had been inspired by the legendary Art Tatum.

He smiled. 'Next time we see each other, I'll play for you.'

But that was not to be. Times spent at Herschel Road were never predictable. As I was walking across the lawn from the swimming pool, I heard raised voices in the drawing room and stopped. I wondered if I should turn back but suspected I had already been seen so continued on to the terrace. Miranda was staying, so I guessed it was an issue concerning her. It was Tess's exasperated voice that I heard first.

'There's nothing I can do, Miranda. He refuses to see you.'

'But he's my father. I've every right to see him,' she shouted.

I winced as I listened to the exchange. Tess reiterated time and again that there was no way Victor was going to come out of his study and Miranda continued protesting vehemently.

'He can't treat me like this. I'm his daughter.'

As she spoke, I caught sight of her stamping her foot and gesticulating with her arms before beginning on another tack. My sympathies lay with them both. I felt compassion for Miranda, whose father was refusing to see her, but also for Tess, who during her marriage must have played the role of intermediary countless times. No wonder she had a nervous twitch. My presence in the doorway did not halt the exchange, but at one point Tess turned to me, looking exhausted and vulnerable, to say that Wally the chauffeur would take me home. It was a relief to leave.

It was not until later that I heard a fuller account of Miranda's story and realised that my suspicions were correct. Her husband, Boudjemaa Boumaza, had been murdered. He was an Algerian political activist who campaigned for the Berbers and had met Miranda at an exhibition in Amsterdam. The reason given for his death was that he was a gun-runner, but few believed it. As my mother had hinted, it was deemed inappropriate for a Moslem to marry a member of the Rothschild family, so he was probably done away with. A grief-stricken Miranda was rescued by her mother Barbara, who took her back to her home in Greece to recover from the shock.

But it was time for me to focus on my course at the Central School. While my father had been working in London, he had shared a flat with his mother, my grandmother. She was a woman of wisdom and integrity whom I liked enormously. She looked older than her years, always dressed in grey, wore her hair tightly pulled back in a bun and had never been concerned about trends or fashion, which was one of the reasons I admired her. Having married a Winchester School housemaster a good deal older than herself, she had been widowed early and moved to London to be closer to my father.

She had five children, four sons and a daughter, my father being the eldest. One of her sons had been killed in the war, another suffered brain damage from a childhood illness and spent the latter part of his life in a mental hospital, and her only daughter had distanced herself from the family. But my grandmother never complained and showed gratitude and appreciation for all that she had. As her flat was close to the Central School, my parents suggested I stay with her. Not only would this save money, but I could also keep an eye on her as she was becoming frail. So we redecorated my father's old room, bought new curtains and cushions, and by September I was ready to start college.

Cutting the Cord

~

My year in Cambridge had changed me. I had more self-confidence, was better able to express myself and looked forward to my course and new life in London. My fellow students were an eclectic group, most of whom aspired to being theatre or television directors, but I had no goal apart from becoming a competent stage manager. The training was like an apprenticeship for life. I learned about electrics, sound, carpentry, lighting, costumes and set design. One moment I was painting flats, the next breaking down furniture or waving sheets of metal to simulate thunder. Each task became an opportunity to master new skills and I enjoyed working alongside those in my year... but there was one in particular I was drawn to. Richard was sensitive, enquiring and there was an immediate connection between us. With him I was able to talk about my fears and aspirations in a way I had never felt able to do before. When we reached out to each other, there was tenderness, a sense of longing, and I knew that he cared, yet there was something that made me hold back. It was only later that I realised why.

Our year had the responsibility of stage-managing plays that were performed by the third-year acting group. This time it was an Ibsen play and I was in charge of electrics. All I had to do was follow instructions and operate a row of levers, but I pulled one up instead of down. I had no idea of the implications of what I had done until I heard one of the actors call out, 'Can I have some light on my entrance?'

It was Martin Potter – and the stage had been plunged into darkness. As agents and directors came to spot new talent in the actors' final year, I felt bad about what I had done, but I got through the play with no more hitches and afterwards escaped to the local pub. Across the bar, I caught sight of Martin with the rest of the cast and summoned up courage to go and apologise.

'There are so many levers and I pulled the wrong one... it was my first time on lighting. I'm sorry.'

'Don't worry. We learn from mistakes. I've made enough of them.'

And without any prompting, he began telling me about himself – how initially he had wanted to become a doctor but had been offered the role of Hamlet in a school play and, owing to its success, his teachers and parents had encouraged him to apply for drama school.

'Lucky to have that support,' I commented, remembering my own experience. 'Where were you at school?'

'Leeds. I'm from Yorkshire. I'm always drawn back there... to the moors, the stone walls and sheep.'

I listened, captivated by Martin's openness and stories about life in the North. In the middle of a conversation about the Brontës' poetry, he broke off to say, 'Do you want come back to my place?'

'Where?'

'West Hampstead... not Yorkshire,' he smiled.

Floral wallpaper, fusty smells and candlewick bedspreads were the norm in North London's bed-sit land. I wondered why I had accepted his invitation so readily, but there was something about Martin that intrigued me. It was not just his penetrating green eyes and hauntingly good looks, but he seemed able to access those parts of me that I tried to keep hidden. Over the years, I had built a wall of protection around myself to ward off criticism and possible rejection. If I let anyone come too close, they might glimpse the real Eliza who was uncertain and afraid. So I was drawn to this man, who wanted to break through my outer defences and discover the real me.

We drank coffee, an excuse for waiting a while, then he took my head in his hands, turned my face towards his and asked, 'Who are you saving yourself for?'

I was an idealist, a romantic and did not want to commit to anyone until I was sure it was the right person... and I had only just met him. I looked into his eyes searching for an answer, touched his cheeks, lips, and he drew me to him and held me tight. I did not want this moment to end. All my life I had been looking for understanding and love, and now I had met someone who could see beyond my fears and insecurities. So I gave myself to him freely, openly, without restraint, believing that my prayers had been answered at last.

Our liaison was noticed by my tutor, who gave me a gentle warning 'not to Potter around the corridors'. I knew that he had my best interest at heart as I had heard about Martin's unpredictability. The course leaders did not want me to lose my sense of direction, career and possibly my independence too. But it was difficult not to be swayed by Martin's obsession. He offered me all that I had longed for in life – to be cherished, wanted and adored. As passion banished reason, I became engulfed by emotions that I had never experienced before. All I wanted was to spend time with him and be cared for, understood and supported.

Within months we were talking about marriage, meeting his parents and he suggested taking me to Yorkshire. The journey north was long and we arrived late, but a spread of sandwiches, cakes, scones and tea were laid ready on the table. His parents received me like a long-lost daughter and I was touched by their welcome. Within the Potter household, there was a feeling of relaxation, ease and belonging that contrasted with the formality of Cambridge life. While there, Martin took me for walks and showed me the landscape that inspired him – moorland, heather, outcrops of rock and sheep sheltering by stone walls. The expanse of countryside offered a sense of freedom that I found invigorating.

On our way home, I suggested a diversion to Cambridge so I could introduce Martin to my parents. I was proud of my new boyfriend and imagined that he and my father would get on well, discussing the theatre and Shakespeare. As I drew up outside the house, however, I felt a twinge of apprehension so suggested that Martin wait in the car until I told them we were here. I found my mother in the kitchen making mayonnaise. She was startled when she saw me and asked what I was doing. I explained that we had just returned from Yorkshire and thought we would drop in.

'Who's "we"?'

'Martin, my new boyfriend.'

'But we've got guests for lunch. It's not convenient.'

'I can set two more places. We can join you.'

'There's no room,' she said quickly.

I could feel my body freeze. I tried a different tack. 'I can help you with lunch. Here, let me finish that.'

'No,' she snapped. 'Leave it alone.'

Her voice was getting louder and her face reddened. I saw the signs and knew that she was on the verge of losing control, but nevertheless I tried again. 'Just meet him at least... please,' I implored.

But that was too much and she yelled the familiar words: 'Get out.'

'Please, Mum—'

'Leave. You'll ruin my lunch party. Get out of this house. Get out. Get out,' she screamed hysterically.

I dared not tell Martin about the reception I had received so ran upstairs to my bedroom, buried my head in my arms and sobbed into the pillow. After a while there was a knock on the door. It was my father, who came in gingerly.

'My dear, I think it's best that you go.'

Why did he always back her up? Why could he never support me? I noticed a look of guilt on his face when he saw my tear-stained face. Then he put his hand on my shoulder to encourage me to get up and shepherded me downstairs. As we went, he muttered something about it being better for everyone if we left.

'Another time maybe…' he mumbled.

He accompanied me down the garden path, but after a few steps turned back. He did not want to risk seeing Martin. Then I ran to the car, gasping for breath between the cries.

'What's happened?' Martin asked, taking me in his arms and wiping the tears from my cheeks.

All I wanted was to get away. So I pulled back from him, started the car and drove off, even though I knew it was unsafe as I was could not see for the tears.

'You can't drive like this,' Martin said, putting his hand on my knee. 'Pull in when you can.'

As soon as we were out of sight, I stopped in a lay-by and broke down, sobbing helplessly. Amidst the cries, I could feel the depth of the pain, the hurt, the sense of outrage that had always been there. And the more aware of it I became, I knew that the umbilical cord between my mother and me had to be cut. By doing so, I would be free… to find my own pathway and take whatever direction I chose.

'We'll manage,' Martin whispered, 'we've got each other so we don't need anyone else.'

My grandmother must have heard about our visit to Cambridge as unexpectedly she suggested that Martin and I spend the Easter holidays with her in Cornwall. She had met him on several occasions and they got on well, so we accepted her invitation, glad there would only be the three of us. I looked forward to showing

Martin the landscape where I had spent my childhood summers. We walked along windswept cliffs, explored hidden coves and caves, watched the gannets feed, and felt the spray on our faces as the waves crashed against the rocks. We had separate bedrooms, so at night Martin would sneak around the house and come in through my bedroom window. But since barbers' shops were closed over Easter, we had no contraceptives and so took risks. Not long after we returned to London, I began feeling nauseous and dizzy. I had no idea what was wrong, but Bob heard I was unwell and arranged for me to see his doctor. I was taken aback when he asked if I could be pregnant.

'I suggest you ask your GP for a test,' the doctor suggested.

'Don't tell Bob.'

'I'll mention glandular fever as a possibility,' he said kindly.

As I stood in the phone kiosk waiting for the result, I felt unexpectedly calm. If it were negative, it would be a relief. If positive, I would regard it as a privilege to be carrying Martin's child. When I was put through to the doctor, he said quietly, 'The test's positive. What will you do?'

'Have the baby,' I said, without any hesitation.

'Well done,' he replied, respecting my choice.

I felt a tingle of excitement and then became overwhelmed as I put my hands on my belly and vowed I would give the child the love I had longed for all my life. I had no fear of telling Martin the news. I knew he would be pleased, despite having this unexpected responsibility when embarking upon his new career. But I trusted we would manage, with or without the support of our parents.

When I phoned my mother to tell her the news, I felt composed. There was a pause and I wondered what her response would be. But to my surprise there was no rebuke or reprimand, just an invitation to go and see them in Cambridge. Unlike my last visit, I was welcomed warmly and my father quickly reassured me that there were no recriminations. Maybe memories of that time had paved the way? As I sat on the sofa looking across at them, I wondered what to expect. My mother began by asking what I intended to do.

'I'm going to have the baby. Martin's asked me to marry him.'

They looked surprised.

'What about adoption?' my mother suggested. 'There are many childless couples who desperately want to be parents. Your baby would be well cared for.'

'But I want to keep it,' I said adamantly, relieved they had not mentioned abortion.

'You've no idea how restrictive it is having a child,' my mother warned. 'You won't be able to run the smallest errand without taking the child along. And what about your career? Are you going to abandon it? You're doing so well.'

'There are plenty of working mothers,' I reminded her.

'So have you decided?' my father intervened.

I nodded and my mother changed tack.

'You'll have to get married quickly. The baby will soon show.'

Of course… for her it was all about appearances, what people would think about her teenage daughter getting pregnant and having to get married in haste.

'You can have a small wedding here,' my mother concluded, 'just family and your godparents, Tess and Alan.'

'Martin's family too,' I added. 'You'll like them. They're pleased, even though there is concern about how it will affect his career. But we won't let it. I'll give Martin all the support I can.'

Within three weeks, a civil ceremony had been arranged with a lunch party afterwards. I bought a red shift dress, Martin chose a gold plaited ring, but there was no financial or practical help from my parents. I did my own hair, forgot to pick some flowers to carry, but it was a fine day which meant we could enjoy a lunch of salmon and salad in the garden. Tension eased over a glass of wine, the two families got on well and had more in common than they expected.

Instead of heading straight back to drama school, Tess suggested we spend our honeymoon night at Rushbrooke. It was a relief to get away and I enjoyed the familiar drive to Suffolk, but the formality of being alone with Martin in the Rothschild house felt strange. As we sat either end of the dining table being served *hors d'oeuvres*, roast chicken followed by strawberries and cream, my mind went back to the times I had been there as a child. I tried to lighten the atmosphere with inconsequential remarks, but neither Martin nor I could relax. When dinner had finished, we escaped to the guest bedroom. It was then that I realised the pathway I had chosen was not going to be easy.

We returned to drama school the following day, Martin to complete his course and me to tell my tutor I would be opting out of my second year. But I got my job back with the Cambridge Theatre Company and Martin was chosen for the lead in their play, so we were assured of income until the baby was born. All we now needed was somewhere to live. As no one in London was prepared to rent accommodation to an actor and teenage mother, we headed for the countryside where a landowner offered us a newly renovated cottage in the grounds of his manor house. The fact that it was in the middle of a field with no vehicular access was of no concern to us.

But we had no furniture nor money to buy it, so Bob decided to help. He liked Martin, sympathised with the position we were in and wanted the baby to have a proper home. So before we moved in, gifts arrived in the form of a fridge, cooker, crockery and other essentials; but Bob was worried how I would fare living in a field.

'I would go mad,' he told Martin. 'What's Eliza going to do?'

'Look after the baby.'

'She'll get bored, you'll see.'

And I knew Bob had touched upon something I was soon going to have to face. I had left my course prematurely, said farewell to my friends and landed myself in the middle of the countryside with only hedgerows to look at.

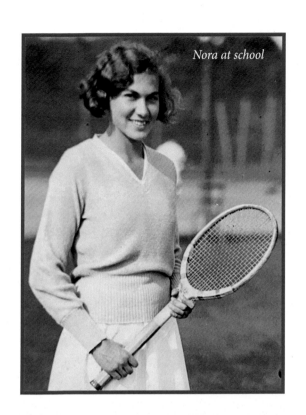

Nora at school

Nora (centre) with friends in Ashby-de-la-Zouche

*Nora at Cambridge
University*

*Dick David in
Alexandria – 1944*

Bob Boothby, the young politician

Dick David (right) with his parents, grandmother, and his wife Nora (centre) pregnant with Eliza – Cornwall 1947

The David Family at Ashton House

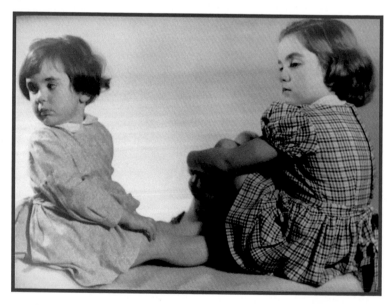

Eliza and Teresa – 1950

Victor Rothschild in his study in Cambridge

Tess Rothschild

Merton Hall School – Eliza second left, Emma second right

Elizabeth and Emma in Wengen

Bob in Montecarlo with Dadie Rylands and Arthur Marshall

Bob in his constituency in Aberdeenshire

Dick, Nora, Nic, Sebastian, Teresa and Eliza at Barton Road, Cambridge – 1963

Martin, Eliza and Rachel – 1969

When the baby was due, it was a relief to move back to my grandmother's flat in London to be close to the hospital. But a big baby and a slight mother resulted in a long labour and a difficult birth. Martin never left my side, remained focussed throughout, encouraging me to take deep breaths and cling on to him. And when Rachel finally arrived, entranced by his new daughter, he took her in his arms and rocked her to and fro. But I was too exhausted to hold her and was glad when the midwife took her off to weigh and measure her and put her in a cot. As I was being stitched up, I glanced across at my daughter and the reality of having a baby to look after hit home. She looked like me, but vulnerable, tiny and she was my responsibility. I was brought back from my reverie by the nurse telling me that I had visitors.

'Who?' I asked in astonishment. It was past eleven o'clock at night.

'It's a surprise.'

The nurse pulled the sheet up over me, opened the door and in came Bob and Teresa with beaming smiles.

'How did you know?' I asked in amazement.

'We called and were told that you'd had a baby girl,' Bob said, walking over to the cot to look at Rachel. Then he turned to me. 'You're a very clever girl. She's beautiful. Did it hurt?'

'A lot. I'm not having any more.'

'You say that now,' the nurse intervened, 'but pain's forgotten quickly. You're young and you'll soon be having another one before you know it.'

I looked across at Teresa, who appeared somewhat over-awed by the sight of the delivery room and me having spent twenty-four hours in labour. It was a lot to take in. She had just returned from New York, where Bob had helped her get a job at Sotheby's for a year. While she was away, I had become pregnant, married Martin and now had a daughter. I suspected that it would not be long before she followed suit. She did not like being left out.

A few days in Cambridge to recuperate left Martin in no doubt that he wanted to find a job well away from my mother.

'It's our child. She's not going to tell us how to bring up Rachel.'

'I won't let her,' I assured him.

'You won't have a choice.'

I knew that he was right. So when Martin was offered a job at the Pitlochry Festival Theatre, he took it without hesitation. With the car piled high with belongings for a year and Rachel in a Moses basket, we set off for Perthshire in Scotland. But on an income of twelve pounds a week, all we could afford was a one-bedroom cottage up a track with no electricity. When we arrived I could not hold back the tears.

'I can't live here. I want to be near people and shops.'

But we never bothered to move. Instead I became accustomed to our house on the hillside. While Martin rehearsed and performed, I took Rachel for walks, listened to the radio, learned to knit, write poetry and became accustomed to spending the days and evenings alone. Nevertheless when I heard that Teresa was coming to stay, I was relieved to have some company.

She told me that she had reconnected with her first boyfriend, Tony, whom she had met in Cornwall at the age of eighteen. He was now living in Wales, reading English at Lampeter University. When she told me that they were planning to marry, I smiled to myself that my suspicions had been proved correct. But, unlike my wedding, Teresa's was going to be a grand occasion with a marquee on the lawn, lunch for a hundred guests followed by a honeymoon in Yugoslavia. The date was set for July, so Rachel and I took an overnight sleeper to London, where my mother collected us. On the way home, she talked enthusiastically about wedding preparations but expressed doubt as to whether Bob should be invited.

'Of course he must,' I said emphatically, 'he's Teresa's godfather, after all.'

'But he may get drunk,' she retorted, 'and then you don't know what he may do.'

Clearly she was worried that he might say something untoward. If it were true that Teresa was Bob's daughter, he might feel drawn to add to my father's speech, express his feelings for his goddaughter, or daughter, and create a scene. Since telling Teresa that he was her father, she had withdrawn from him. Tony also had little time for him but did have a high regard for my father, with whom he shared interests in classics, music and botany. So I waited and watched, curious to see what would happen on the day.

The morning of the wedding, I was delighted to hear that Bob was on his way. Teresa looked radiant in a silk white mini dress with buttons down the back and welcomed guests with her customary social flare. When my father began his speech, I looked across at Bob and noticed that he was listening attentively to every word that my father said. And when the toast was made, he raised his glass high to cheer the couple on with a smile on his face. He was proud to see his favourite godchild begin her new life as a married woman. He clearly loved her for who she was and had no need to draw attention to himself, or interrupt the proceedings.

It was a relief to get back to Pitlochry. I had grown accustomed to the quietness of life in the Scottish Highlands and my walks through fields and forests. The joy of being with Rachel now surpassed anything I could have imagined. She was crawling, beginning to talk and every moment I spent with her seemed like a sublime gift. But just four weeks after Teresa's wedding, I had unexpected guests.

'Hello, anyone there?'

At once I recognised Bob's resonant voice. I opened the door and there he was with Gordon and an elegantly dressed woman with long dark hair.

'My treasure,' Bob said, using his familiar endearment. 'This is Wanda. I married her yesterday at the Caxton Hall.'

I offered my congratulations, invited them in and told them that Martin was still in bed.

'Get up, Martin. We're here for breakfast,' Bob hollered.

Martin appeared in his pyjamas. 'This is an unexpected surprise.'

'It's the first day of our honeymoon and we've come to celebrate it with you.' Bob beamed. 'We're starving. We came up on the night train. What have you got to eat?'

'Not much,' I said, looking at the remains of a loaf of bread.

'I'll go and get some bacon and eggs,' Gordon offered, and disappeared out of the door.

When he returned he cooked a full English breakfast, which Bob and Martin topped off with a nip of whisky. As we ate, Bob was ebullient and explained that he had met Wanda in the south of France a few years ago and had immediately fallen in love with her. Since then he had asked her to marry him on numerous occasions and finally she had agreed. At their wedding crowds of journalists and admirers had come to wish them well. Privileged that they had chosen to spend the first day of their honeymoon with us, I asked why they had come to Scotland.

'I wanted to show Wanda the place of my birth and introduce her to the fishermen and famers I've represented in Parliament for more than forty years.'

And I recalled the deep love he had for his homeland and felt glad that I was spending time here too.

Inner Journeying

As the season at Pitlochry came to an end, I dreaded the idea of returning to the field in the South. I wanted more stimulus, not just for me but Rachel too. So when a friend told me that he had a two-bedroomed flat to rent in London, I wasted no time in agreeing a deal. It suited Martin too. During our last weeks in Scotland, he had approached a number of theatre directors and agents that led to him being offered a part at the Hampstead Theatre Club. But with his charismatic looks and enigmatic presence, I sensed his future lay on screen rather than the stage. So with this in mind I encouraged him to have some photos taken that resulted in a folio of compelling portraits, which were soon being circulated among casting directors all over the world. It was only a matter of weeks before Martin was asked to meet Federico Fellini, an Italian film director, who was looking for a young man to play the lead in his new film, *Satyricon*. An interview led to a screen test, followed by an invitation to lunch with the producer, and within a few weeks, Martin was offered the part of Encolpius.

However, filming was to take place at the *Cinecitta* film studios near Rome and was scheduled to take nine months. As I wondered how this would impact upon our family life, Martin told me his plans.

'I'm going alone,' he said in a matter-of-fact voice.

His words cut through me like a knife.

'What about Rachel?' I asked, attempting to divert the attention away from myself.

Ignoring me, he continued: 'It's an opportunity of a lifetime and I don't want any distractions. I have to do this on my own.'

In one brief exchange, it felt as though I had been dismissed from his life. There was no discussion as his decision was final. My task was to readjust to the news.

I could understand that he did not want to be constrained by a wife and child but have the freedom to immerse himself in his role and whatever was required of him. After all, that was the nature of Fellini's films – portraying the extremes of life and the multifarious dreams of humanity – and *Satyricon* was no exception. When it was time for Martin leave, the parting was tender and poignant. I hid my tears, wished him well, but as soon as he was gone, I developed excruciating sinus pain to the point where I could hardly walk. I knew it was an expression of the hurt and sense of loss I felt deep inside and it took time before it eased. My twenty-first birthday came and went... alone, my one consolation being some trinkets Martin sent from Italy. Not long afterwards, however, there was an invitation for Rachel and me to join him for Christmas.

The elegant chaos of the capital city, with its bustling streets and heightened emotions, engulfed me as soon as I arrived. Martin seemed genuinely pleased to see me and my fear about feeling unwelcome quickly faded away. He told me of his idea of first spending time in Rome to show me the sights and then going to Spoleto for Christmas, where we could walk in the hills. He had also arranged for a friend to look after Rachel in the evenings so we could eat out together.

'Tonight we're going to Ceserina's on Fellini's recommendation. He says she makes the best pasta in Italy. Hiram's coming too.'

Hiram Keller was an American actor, who was playing the

part of Ascyltus, Martin's rebellious young friend. The two of them filmed by day and went out together at night. Over a bowlful of *tagliatelle al tartufo*, they entertained me with stories about Fellini's macabre circus of characters and his portrayal of life in Rome in pre-Christian times.

Hiram explained, 'Without any spiritual values, the rich and powerful could indulge their insatiable appetite for sex, food and games, so that's what Fellini expects of us too.'

I glanced across at Martin.

'Why not come to *Cinecitta* tomorrow, Eliza?' Hiram suggested. 'We're filming the Garden of the Suicides. Sounds morbid, but it's a moving story.'

'What's it about?' I asked.

'A nobleman and his wife are about to have their property and land seized by Caesar. They can't bear the humiliation, so they free their slaves, send their children away to safety and then make a pact to take their own life. Lucia Bose plays the *matrona*. It would be a chance to see Fellini film and you can bring Rachel too. There are plenty of crew who'll be glad to look after her.'

And I was glad that Hiram included me.

The studio taxi picked us up at four in the morning. It was the same daily routine for Martin: first weight training to build up his muscles, an hour or two in hair and make-up, then time spent with his script, followed by breakfast before filming began. While he was occupied, one of the producers showed me around the film studios, explaining the different sets that had been built specifically for the film, each one as big as a theatre. When Fellini arrived, there was a hush before filming began. I listened as Fellini's mesmeric voice talked the actors through the scene as the camera slowly moved across their faces… first the husband and wife, then the servants and lastly the children. Little seemed to be happening so I edged closer. This time, as the camera lingered on each face, I watched Fellini look intently at each actor, quietly coaxing from them the emotion that he desired – sadness, loss, innocence, the pain of parting and death... yes, I began to see the subtlety of his art and how the actors merged with their role.

For Fellini, Martin and Encolpius were one – the handsome blue-eyed youth, lover of men and women, someone who lived life on the edge, unafraid of embracing life's extremes. He was an adventurer, poet and philosopher, willing to embrace the dark as well as the light and discover all that the world has to offer.

One evening Martin confided, 'Fellini expects me to experience all sides of life in Rome.'

'What do you mean?' I asked apprehensively.

'He wants me to go to all-night parties, experiment with drugs, prostitutes, gay relationships... you name it...' Then after a pause he added, '...but I have you and Rachel.'

I remained silent.

'I feel torn,' Martin continued. 'I want to make the most of the opportunity Fellini has given me. It's a pivotal point in my career and I don't want to feel held back.'

I waited a moment before replying, 'We were so young when we got married, Martin. I don't think I ever expected to keep you for myself. You're too good-looking for that. But one thing I've learned is that being truthful with one another always brings us closer. So all I ask is that you don't deceive me. I couldn't bear that. Just be honest about what you are doing and who you are drawn to.'

So he began telling me about the time when he had been with a high-class prostitute from the Via Veneto, parties where he had watched gay sex and his experiences with drugs. His openness brought us closer and mitigated some of the hurt I felt as he strayed into uncharted territory. But it took courage on both our parts to face the truth and relinquish the need for self-protection.

Inspired by what I had seen at *Cinecitta*, when I returned to England I picked up the camera I had exchanged for my Brownie Box and began taking pictures. I learned how to process film, print photographs and master the full tonal range that black and white photography had to offer. In this way I could capture nuances of expression and the different moods of a landscape. I began taking portraits of actors, friends, the old and the young. It was an opportunity to be still, engage with someone at a deeper level and reveal the story that was held in a face. But by accessing the feelings of others, I realised that I was avoiding my own, as in truth I felt lost and alone. Martin's success reflected back to me a sense of inadequacy and failure that had haunted me all my life.

This became more acute with the completion of the Fellini film, as it heralded a new beginning in his career. The star of the Fellini film was wanted for interviews, photo shoots and articles in magazines. New films took him on location to Denmark, Spain and the island of Bali, and on stage he performed in London before going on tour. I became aware of waves of envy sweeping through me, from which there was no escape.

Days were long… and nights too, especially when he was out until daybreak and I lay in bed waiting and wondering what he was up to. I no longer knew where my own path lay. Apart from photography, I had no resources to fall back on. I had given up my career and was restricted by a toddler who needed my care. So by way of taking some control over my life, one day I decided not to have toast and my mother's homemade marmalade for breakfast. Then I began limiting myself to salad for lunch and gradually fell into a pattern of reducing my food intake more and more. On occasion I had hunger pains, but I did not mind as I felt lighter, so then I tried missing meals altogether. I was not overweight, but I imagined that I would look more attractive if my figure was better honed as I now had to compete with Martin's leading ladies.

As my weight dropped, I became aware of an inner reality that felt more authentic than the outer world, which increasingly seemed like a passing dream. Pursuing a pathway of self-denial gave me a sense of empowerment, made me feel different from the crowd, like a witness who was able to watch the antics of the world without being a part of it. I began questioning people's preoccupation with their role, image and appearance, instead of asking the more important questions such as: Who am I? What is my destiny, and that of the planet too? I sought answers from mystical poets like Shelley, Keats and Yeats, and read Plato's theory about the world of ideas being a truer reality than that of physicality and form. Sometimes it felt as though a wildness, a madness was taking hold of me, but it felt exhilarating and I had no fear. I realised why spiritual paths used asceticism as a pathway to self-realisation, as the less I ate, the clearer my vision became. By denying the body, my mind was becoming freer.

'How little food does one need to survive?' I asked my brother, who was the doctor.

'Very little, a bit of starch and some vegetables and pulses. We all eat too much.'

So I had the answer I wanted. We all overindulge.

My sister had just had her second child, so I went to stay with her to help. As she watched me wade through a pile of ironing, she commented on how thin I looked. I mentioned I had not had a period for four or five months and wondered why.

'Are you pregnant?' she asked.

'No, I don't feel it anyway.'

'Maybe it's your weight,' she said. 'A friend of mine became anorexic and stopped menstruating. You should eat more. Once anorexia takes hold, it's difficult to turn it around...' and her voice trailed off.

I listened but found it difficult to absorb what she said. The world had taken on a different hue, one in which everything scintillated – colours were richer, leaves danced on the trees and light shone through pebbles on a seashore. My new reality had become my refuge and I did not want it to change. But one evening, when I was getting ready to host a drinks party to celebrate Martin's first night of *Hamlet*, I had a bath to freshen up and could not sit down as my bones were protruding too much. When I got out, I stood naked in front of the mirror and for the first time saw my wasted, skeletal frame. I no longer looked like a woman but more like someone out of Belsen. Although Martin knew I was unwell, he could not cope and had no idea what to do, so I knew I was on my own. And to my surprise I found myself reaching out to my mother.

'I'm not well, Mum. I need help.'

'Come home, my darling, come home. We've been so worried about you.'

I could hear relief in my mother's voice. I still had no answers, but I knew that time was running out. When I returned to Cambridge, familiar surroundings mirrored back to me the person I had become. With clarity I could see my habits and the impact they were having on those around me. I concealed food, destroyed it, lied about it, did anything rather than eat it, despite all the care that had gone into preparing and cooking it. I wanted to turn the tide but did not know how to do it. As I became increasingly disgusted by myself, I reached out to my father for help.

'I have nothing to offer the world, no talent, no means of self-expression… nothing. I don't know what to do.'

He was thoughtful and then began reassuring me. 'You're a good mother and loyal wife. That means a lot. Picasso was a genius, but he wasn't a contented man. I admire those who find happiness without excelling at any one thing. I believe they are the greater men and women.'

I found comfort in his words and sensed they might be self-reflective and true of himself.

My mother booked me an appointment with a consultant who specialised in anorexia. Among Cambridge University students, eating disorders were not unusual, so it was known as one of the best places for treatment. Without delay, I was admitted to hospital weighing just thirty kilos. I now had to make a choice – to eat or let myself slip away. I had no fear of death as I knew my journey would carry on but, if I wanted to find answers to the questions that were stirring within me, I had to get well and live. I also had Rachel to care for. So with the doctor's help, I made every effort to eat, minimally increasing my calorie intake daily and resting after each meal. After a month or so, my metabolic rate increased, my body filled out and I began to feel like a woman again.

During my stay in hospital, my parents looked after Rachel and to my surprise, seemed to enjoy having a two-year-old running around the house. When I was discharged, I sat on the terrace with a cup of tea and a digestive biscuit, while watching my father with Rachel. I was taken aback when I saw him hold her hand, twirl her around, before taking her to pick apples and sweep up leaves. He looked years younger. That evening my mother told me that he blamed himself for my anorexia.

'It was nothing to do with him, nor Martin for that matter,' I assured her. 'It was my own journey, to find the truth of myself, but I'm sure there are better ways of doing that.'

I doubted if my mother understood what I was saying, but it did not matter. She listened and went on to say how much my father had enjoyed Rachel being here and now thought of her as his daughter.

It was a time for new beginnings. I now wanted Martin to have his freedom and for me to have mine. Excited once more by the future, I began looking for a property in London for Rachel and me, and it did not take long to find a beautiful Georgian house in Chiswick with views of the Thames. But with four bedrooms it was too large and it also needed renovating, a task that I did not want to take on myself. So Martin came to see it, fell in love with it and suggested we buy it and do it up together. I realised that I was giving in too easily, but it was difficult not to be swayed by his persuasive powers. I told myself that if we that if we focussed on design, paint colours and wood finishes, a new bond would grow between us. The garden needed taming too and Martin liked physical work. But we could only afford to buy if I drew upon the trust money that Bob had given me. When we told him of our plans, without hesitation, he arranged for sufficient funds to be released, saying that owning a house was the best investment we could make.

'So why haven't you done it yourself?' I teased.

'Because the gambling tables, whisky, good food and company take precedence,' he laughed.

As the house took on a semblance of order, we began to entertain friends. One evening John Vere Brown, whose photographs of Martin had caught Fellini's attention, came to supper. The conversation revolved around the latest television dramas, forthcoming theatre productions and what work other actors were doing. I knew Martin found such conversations threatening, believing he should be doing more himself. I noticed John observing him, sensing his unease. Then unexpectedly he made a suggestion.

'I've just learned to meditate. Why not try it, Martin? It helps release tension.'

I pricked up my ears, not because of the potential benefit to Martin, but the word 'meditation' struck a chord within me. It was as though I had just been handed a key to myself, a means of accessing those parts of me that I had been trying for years to reach.

'Robert taught me,' John continued. 'He said it would help reduce my blood pressure. He's just got back from a three-month teacher-training course with Maharishi and is looking for students.'

'How does it work?' I asked, intrigued.

'It's something you have to experience. It can't be described in words.'

As I opened the door of a darkened North London room, it was like entering another world. Candles were lit, camphor burning and the sweet smell of incense filled the air. I handed Robert gifts of fresh fruit and wildflowers, which he carefully placed on the *puja* table. Then softly he began singing Sanskrit prayers and making offerings of water and rice. Lulled by his chanting and the ambience of the room, I slipped into a dream-like state, and after a while, Robert turned to me and whispered my mantra.

'Feel its vibration resonate within you.'

In the following days my horizons expanded. I was not sure whether it was the experience of meditation or discovering there were other dimensions and higher states of consciousness that could be accessed when our minds were clear. Disconnected events came together in a glorious kaleidoscope of colour and symmetry as the jigsaw puzzle of my life began to take shape. During the following months, I never missed a meditation. It was a sanctuary, one that opened up a new reality that was limitless, mysterious and filled with potential. Instead of feeling imprisoned in a three-dimensional world, I was now able to see the underlying unity of all. As images and ideas came into my mind, I took up my pen and began expressing them in poetry and prose. I wanted to share my realisations, but with whom? Martin was preoccupied with himself and his career, my parents were suspicious of esoteric ideas, Bob's panacea was whisky… so I reached out to Victor, who was intrigued to hear my thoughts about humanity and the world.

VICTOR

~

'So are we strands of purest woven light?' Victor probed.

He had just read my poem '*Is It a Perfect Dream...*', a story about a speck of light that travels through different solar systems and galaxies, experiencing a multitude of lifetimes, until finally it finds its home at the centre of the Universe.

'Perhaps that's our journey, but none of us know,' I replied. 'I imagine, I dream and in my mind go beyond time and space. This three-dimensional reality is so limiting. We're imprisoned in a box, always looking for a way out.'

Victor listened, curious to find out more about my ideas on life, death and our destiny.

I continued: 'I want to peel back our outer defences to find our essence, the truth of who we are. When my body was wasting away, consciousness expanded and I perceived the subtlest levels of form and physicality – vibrant colours and iridescent light. We're just bands of frequency vibrating at different levels and we've come here to Earth to play, explore and learn how to transcend the illusions of this world. Don't you feel you've been here before?'

Victor side-stepped the question. 'You have vision. None of my children have vision. That's why I enjoy being with you.'

I was surprised and looked away, not sure how to respond. Then I cast my mind through his six offspring, aware of all their successes and achievements. I was all too aware of their vast intellectual capability that was expressed through different disciplines – economics, history, English and the arts. I could not compare myself with any of them and told Victor so.

'Awareness is different from intelligence,' he replied. 'I have an exceptionally high IQ, but having vision is a gift.'

I remained silent, absorbing his words.

'Your mother doesn't have vision,' Victor added.

On that we were agreed. I had always noticed that within the political arena she was always more comfortable following others' ideas, instead of taking the initiative herself. She was now busy climbing the political ladder, proud of being a Cambridge counsellor and sitting on numerous committees. Victor's perception of my mother prompted me to ask more.

'What was she like when she was at university?'

'Sexy and sexual.'

He looked me in the eye as if to gauge my response. I was not shocked as I recognised that it was probably true. I had seen a photograph of her when she was young, standing in a swimsuit amongst a group of friends. Her figure, poise and smile exuded sexuality. She would have no problem capturing the attention of any man.

Victor continued: 'Your mother was not only attractive but sociable too. She could be relied upon to liven up any dull dinner party. Times were different then... we gave ourselves more freedom. For example, I had an agreement with Tess that we could both have affairs.'

I was surprised by his comment and presumed he was hinting that it may have been the same for my mother. Perhaps it was the norm in marriages of that era? After all, they were post Bloomsbury Group, when freedom was associated with sexual liberation. However, I had never felt any sexual innuendoes in

Victor's relationship with me. I had always felt safe with him, free to explore feelings and ideas without being judged or dismissed.

So his flat in St James's Place became my refuge. I visited him once a week and spent the evening there. Times together followed a similar pattern. I arrived around six, took the lift to his third-floor flat and he was always there to welcome me and walk me through to the sitting room, where he offered me a drink. The side table was well stocked with gin, whisky, mixes and soft drinks, but he knew I liked wine. I then sat on the sofa opposite him and, after a brief exchange of news, he played the piano for me. I had little experience of jazz but knew enough to realise that he was an accomplished player. As his fingers moved deftly across the keyboard, I became mesmerised by the music and enjoyed listening to his new creations. At the end, he asked me what I thought and I would always tell him how impressed I was.

'Listen to Art Tatum,' he kept saying. 'He was a genius and I respect geniuses.'

Then he would take me for a simple but delicious dinner at a nearby restaurant.

Over the years, Victor's work had taken him from researching spermatozoa at Cambridge to working for Royal Dutch Shell, but now he was Director of the Central Review Board, also known as the Think Tank. Set up by Prime Minister Edward Heath, it was an independent body within the Cabinet office responsible for developing long term strategy and policy.

'So who governs the country?' I asked. 'Is it the politicians or you?'

'Power never resides with the politicians,' Victor answered matter-of-factly.

His response did not surprise me. I recalled Bob saying it was not the politicians but civil servants in Whitehall who pulled the strings, which is why he had never sought high office.

I changed tack so that I could glean more information: 'Within the Think Tank, who do you admire the most?'

'William Waldegrave without a doubt – he's highly intelligent, good company and the son of an earl. I wish he were my son-in-law.'

'Is there any chance of that?'

'There may be… if Tory plays her cards right.'

I had not seen Victoria, Emma's younger sister, for many years. But I knew that she was attractive, drawn to English literature and the theatre, and enjoyed the company of actors and playwrights. I doubted it would suit her being married to a politician. But for Victor his offspring were the Rothschild gene pool, which not only had to be protected but also enhanced. It was not just the family name but the bloodline too, so his children's choice of spouses was critical.

Nevertheless I teased him: 'You can't arrange marriages for your children. Let love be their guide. You don't own them.'

He smiled, knowing the truth of what I had said, but Victor had an all-consuming need to control, not just his family and friends but the political arena too, which was why his present job suited him well. I presumed our relationship succeeded because he neither wanted nor expected anything from me.

Since the renovation work on our Chiswick house had been completed, Martin had fallen back into his habit of having an occasional fling with women he was working with. John Vere Brown had been right about Martin being thwarted by feelings of insecurity, which resulted in him seeking assurance from women who found him attractive. I weathered the storms by asking him to be honest with me. And when he confessed to his betrayals, there was a softness and gentleness about his demeanour that made me love him all the more. Once again, truthfulness made it easier for me to forgive him and helped us regain the closeness that we once enjoyed. But eventually his ongoing infidelity took its toll and my self-esteem plummeted once again. So it was a relief when he told me he was taking a room with John Taylor, an eminent QC who owned a large house in central London. He had a prestigious clientele and was married to a cousin of my father. But he was also an eccentric and a party lover, so having a celebrated actor as one of his coterie suited him well.

I was on reprieve for a while. No longer did I have to concern myself where Martin was, or who he was with, and my new-found freedom gave me the chance of pursuing interests of my own. I wanted to unravel the mystery of meditation, explore the secrets of mantra and breath, and discover how we could fulfil our true potential. The easiest way of doing this was by learning to be a meditation teacher, which entailed attending a three-month training course in Belgium with Maharishi. And as nursery school facilities were provided, I could take Rachel with me. So I sold my car, rented out a couple of rooms in the house to raise the necessary funds and within a month, we set off across the Channel.

The course was rigorous. Not only did we have extended meditation and yoga sessions, but we also had to study Vedic philosophy, learn to chant prayers in Sanskrit and memorise an exact teaching procedure that allowed students to experience effortless meditation. We also had a succession of tests to get through if we were to become qualified teachers. At the end of the course, Maharishi came to meet his new initiates and pass on the *bija* mantras that we would use in our teaching. I was curious to meet this small, scantily clad Indian guru with thinning grey hair and an infectious giggle. As he made his way up the aisle of the conference room, students waited their turn to give him flowers, garland him and greet him with *Namaste*.

As I watched the spectacle, my mind went back to The Beatles' experience in India three years before. They too had been won over by Maharishi, inspired by his meditation practice and teachings, but later found out that he was not all that he claimed to be. Maharishi gave the impression that he was celibate, but on occasion had made sexual advances towards women, one of whom was the actress

Mia Farrow. John Lennon recorded his feelings of betrayal in a song called 'Sexy Sadie'. But as I recalled these stories, I reminded myself that it was not the man but his teaching that mattered. And as I listened to Maharishi sharing his spiritual insights with clarity and humour, I felt indebted to him as meditation had changed the course of my life.

I noticed there was a small circle of teachers who were with Maharishi at all times, whether travelling, teaching or exploring ideas as to how he could further his mission. The day after Maharishi's arrival one of them approached me, a tall, well-spoken Englishman.

'I'd like to introduce myself, Eliza. I'm Guy, one of Maharishi's helpers. He has expressed a wish to meet you.'

'Why?' I asked in surprise.

'We've heard that you know people in Britain who have influence. Maybe they could help Maharishi get his message to the world?'

I presumed they had heard that my mother was in politics, or that I was acquainted with the Director of the Policy Review Board, but I knew it was unlikely that meditation would get a mention in the Think Tank or Parliament. Nevertheless, I did not want to miss out on the opportunity of meeting Maharishi personally, so I expressed my willingness to help and was invited to attend his morning audience. As I waited in silence with a small group of devotees, I stared at the empty chair in front of me where Maharishi was about to sit, wondering what I had let myself in for. Soon the door handle turned and Maharishi was ushered into the room by two women. We all stood up, before dropping to our knees, and I noticed some of those present went into a full prostration. I felt uncomfortable with this exaggerated display of reverence and was relieved when we sat down.

Maharishi's first words were, 'Where is the English lady?'

'I'm here, Maharishi.'

'Get the lady a chair. The rest of you can go,' he said, waving his hand to dismiss the others. I felt more at ease with Maharishi alone. He began asking me how the course was going, wanting assurance that I understood how the practice worked and that I had learned the teaching procedure thoroughly. He then went on to explain how important it was that meditation was practised in schools, universities, hospitals and businesses. I was surprised that he asked me nothing about myself, nor about the changes that I had experienced since learning the practice. Clearly he was only interested in any influence I might have within the political world.

'I'll make a video for your friends who are in positions of power, explaining the benefits of meditation. If meditation is integrated into the political system from the top, then it can be introduced as a matter of course into everyone's lives.'

I agreed with him in principle, realising that it would be a waste of time explaining that we live in a free society and have an element of choice. But I reassured him that I would show the video to those I thought might be interested.

'And please teach your friends to meditate too.'

I smiled to myself at the thought of Victor bearing gifts of flowers and fruit and receiving a mantra. Then suddenly, as though Maharishi had run out of things to say, he tilted his head on one side, smiled and said, 'Good. I think that's all.'

Suddenly the interview had come to an end. Prior to our meeting I had been instructed not to look into his eyes, as I was told that this drains his energy. I never understood this as we had been told that Maharishi was a man with abundant energy, who only needed a couple of hours' sleep a night. But this had not been an issue, as Maharishi had barely glanced in my direction during the whole conversation.

During our three months away, Martin had not been in touch, although I had written to him weekly giving news of the course and Rachel. At times I sunk low as familiar feelings of hurt and rejection surfaced again. So I was surprised when at the end of the course I received a letter from him, asking when we were coming home and saying he would like to meet us. When Rachel and I arrived, he embraced us warmly as though nothing untoward had happened while we were away. Then he stepped back to take a look at me.

'You look exhausted. What on earth have they been doing to you?'

His comment surprised me, not about me looking tired, but that he cared. I told him that the teacher training had been challenging. I had lost weight and stopped menstruating again, but I had been assured this can happen as the metabolic rate drops when doing extended meditations. After driving us home, he cooked a meal and apologised for not being in touch.

When we were alone together, I asked the question that was uppermost in my mind. 'You've been having an affair, haven't you?'

He looked away before speaking. 'It's over now. Your letters were moving. Each time one arrived, I questioned what I was doing. I couldn't write back as I didn't know what to say. I'm sorry,' he murmured quietly.

I did not pursue the subject further, but during the evening explained my idea of setting up a West London Meditation Centre and running it from home. To my surprise, he was supportive. He seemed relieved, explaining that theatre and film work were now less reliable. He also asked if he could move back home so he could help with Rachel and my teaching, saying it would be a fresh start for us both. Although I had doubts, a sense of peace spread through me, glad that I was still wanted by the man I had fallen in love with when I was just eighteen years old.

But my first responsibility was to pass on the video that Maharishi had made for Victor.

'So did the little man impress you?' he asked.

'I had time alone with him, thanks to you. But it was strange.'

'In what way?'

'Formal, peremptory… his closest disciples treat him like a saint, which made me feel uncomfortable.'

Then I told him about the video in which Maharishi talked about the benefits of meditation. I doubted that he would watch it, but at least I had fulfilled my promise and passed it on. To my surprise, the next time I saw Victor, he said he had watched it and asked if meditation would help people who worked in a biscuit factory.

'Yes, they would have greater job satisfaction,' I replied confidently.

'Why?' Victor asked.

'Because they would be less stressed and experience greater creative energy.'

'In that case, they would no longer be content packing biscuits.'

To that, I had no answer.

Victor continued with his line of thought: 'In the future, boring jobs will be done by robots.'

'Then there will be unemployment,' I replied.

'Systems will be put in place to prevent that.'

I wondered what he meant and imagined that Victor had worked out a way of managing humanity and the world. But before I had a chance to question him further, he brought the conversation to a close, saying he wanted to take me for supper at Wiltons, an exclusive restaurant close to his flat. When we arrived, we were greeted warmly and shown to Victor's favourite table. Since learning to meditate I had become vegetarian, which suited me well as I still had a strange relationship with food. But Victor was understanding, saying he appreciated simple, well-cooked food himself.

'There's a particularly good omelette they serve here. It's filled with spinach and béchamel sauce. I'll order it for us both and we'll have a glass of Sancerre to go with it.'

When the dish arrived, the combination of tastes and texture was sublime. Over supper, Victor asked whether Martin had behaved while I was away and I smiled to myself at Victor's knack of always going straight to the point.

'He wandered... as expected, but apparently the relationship has burned itself out. He never got in touch while I was away, which I found hard. But now he wants to move back home and support my teaching. He's getting less work, so the extra income will be useful.'

'Do you need financial help?'

'I don't want to be dependent upon anyone anymore. That's what has kept me a prisoner all these years. I want to be free of the need of having someone to look after me.'

Shortly after this conversation, I received a letter from Victor with a cheque for two hundred pounds. His message was simple: *I thought this might help.* I was confused. Owing to my wish to be financially independent, I knew that I could not accept the gift, so I tore up the cheque and wrote to explain my decision. A few days later I received a letter of apology, saying he had not meant to offend me. I was touched by his humility, a quality that I had rarely seen in my own family or their circle of friends. But I found the gesture of refusing money empowering and with enthusiasm I threw myself into the task of creating a successful meditation centre – giving talks at the local library before teaching clients the practice. Before long, I was attracting students from all walks of life, who were seeking to increase their vitality, enhance their creativity and reduce stress levels. As growing numbers of people came to learn, not only did my income increase but I also earned a reputation for being a competent and well-respected teacher.

But despite the success of the new West London Teaching Centre, there was still a part of me that felt vulnerable. Despite meditation and inner journeying, I had not managed to dispel a long-held need to be cherished and appreciated so, in my relationship with Martin, I adopted a pattern of appeasement so that I would be the recipient of his love. And into this tangled web

Abi was conceived, which I regarded as a miracle as I believed that anorexia had left me infertile.

But with the prospect of birth and new life came the hope that we would find fulfilment together at last.

TO THE NORTH

~

I was only allowed to hold Abi for a few moments before she was taken to intensive care. As we had different blood groups, my antibodies had been passed on to her so she had to be watched closely. For the next few days, I moved between the special care unit and the ward, feeding and spending time with her when I could. Seeing her in the incubator, she seemed like a study of perfection, one of innocence and beauty.

'She's in heaven,' the nurse commented.

'Wishing she was still there, no doubt,' I smiled.

Martin was away filming *Robin Hood* for a BBC series, and when he did get back, he became irritated by Abi and me still being in hospital.

'Why can't you discharge yourself? She's not in the incubator anymore.'

'The doctor says it's too risky,' I explained. 'What if something happens?'

Martin was already feeling the constraints of having a second child.

When we finally got home, the atmosphere was tense and I looked for an escape. My refuge was going to the local library and leafing through books of black and white photographs of the Lake

District. I dreamed of moving somewhere far away, where I would no longer be the target of Martin's unpredictable moods. During the eleven years we had been married, we had talked about the idea of me living in the country and him being in a flat in London. We had looked at a couple of properties in Cornwall and Wales, but I was drawn to the North – to dales, mountains and lakes. But the reality of taking two children to a place where I had never been and knew no one, would be a challenge... one I that was not sure I was ready to take.

So I chose the path of least resistance and persisted in doing everything I could to please Martin in order to maintain a sense of calm while nursing Abi. I rarely said what I thought and avoided any mention of Martin's work as this always triggered acrimony. Once again I found myself living in the shadow of my own fear and increasingly despised myself for it. I was also aware that Rachel could see through my failing act and Abi was picking up on the tension too. So when a friend told me about an Indian teacher who was offering practices to neutralise fear and open our hearts to love, I was drawn to find out more. The techniques Guruji taught were personally prescribed as he recognised that we all walk different paths. So I wasted no time in contacting him, and within a few weeks, I received a personal mantra, a couple of other practices and a warning about not being gullible... and Guruji added: *Welcome home, my beloved.*

Over the next few months, my life turned upside down. The first change I made was to give up teaching for Maharishi as I could no longer follow the rules of his organisation. Over the years, I had taught people who could not afford the required fee and others who had mental health problems, neither of which was allowed. Honesty was now of paramount importance, not just in my teaching but my personal life too.

'I've decided to leave,' I told Martin one evening. 'I'm going to move north.'

He did not conceal his shock, so I continued before he could say anything.

'I know it'll be a challenge, but it's one I'm prepared to take. For years you've been saying that I am the cause of all your frustration, so by taking myself away, you'll be free.'

He was silent while he absorbed the news. My portrayal of the situation had surprised him as I had taken the blame myself rather than projecting it upon him. I could see confusion in his eyes, but after a while he asked calmly where I would go.

'I've found a house called Woman's Land on the western edge of the Yorkshire Dales. I want to go and see it. It'll mean selling up here, but we'll have made a profit because of the renovation work we've done.'

'But you'll be so far away,' he said in a wistful voice.

'You'll soon find someone else.'

And from the look on his face, I wondered if he already had someone in mind.

My next task was to tell my parents. I imagined my father would be pleased as he often visited the Yorkshire Dales as it was one of his favourite places for flowers. But when I told him of my plans, he put two fingers to his lips in a characteristic manner, shook his head and remained silent. As for my mother, she was at a loss to understand how I could take myself off to such a remote place, so far away from a metropolis.

'You'll never find another husband up there,' was her first remark.

'I'm moving away from my husband, not trying to find another one.'

'What about the children? What will they do in the middle of nowhere?'

'They'll be in the countryside. They'll love it.'

'But you'll have no friends, no access to the theatre, the arts...'

I tried to reassure her that I was neither looking for a social life nor another profession, but I knew that my words were in vain.

Teresa offered to drive me north to see Woman's Land and I was surprised how far north it was. But instantly I fell in love with the white-washed farmhouse and its setting in the lush green valley of Dentdale. When I returned home, Martin had begun looking for one-bedroomed flats in Chelsea and it became apparent there was already another woman on the scene. So we agreed to put the house on the market and within a month we had an offer from Michael Billington, the drama and arts correspondent for *The Guardian*. Delighted that he would be the beneficiary of our work, we agreed a price and it was then time to say my farewells.

I did not have many friends in London as Martin had developed a dislike of anyone visiting the house. So I went to see Bob to explain why I was moving north and that the trust money would be transferred to my new house. Since his marriage to Wanda, I had seen less of him. Whenever I phoned, it was Wanda who answered and she always seemed reluctant to pass me on to Bob. My mother had found the same and none of us were sure if it were her way of protecting Bob, or that she wanted to keep him for herself. She had now taken on many of Gordon's duties – cooking, cleaning and ensuring Bob was immaculately turned out when making his daily appearance at the House of Lords. But when we did come together, times together were easy and enjoyable, although there were hints from Bob that Wanda was now in charge.

'She says I have to cut down my whisky consumption.'

'That's because she loves you and wants to keep her husband,' I teased.

But on another occasion, I heard Bob telling Wanda that she was drinking too much which made her volatile, so I guessed that each projected their own weaknesses onto the other. Yet despite the thirty-year age difference, it was apparent they adored one another and Wanda would not hear a word said against her husband. Bob had found happiness at last. For this reason I never talked about my marriage problems, nor revealed the truth of why I had chosen to live so far away. He liked Martin and they had always got on well and Bob was now seventy-six – the same age as the year – so I did not want to burden him with my own problems.

When I told Victor of my plans, he became distant and withdrew. I knew he was sad that we would no longer have our times together. And characteristically he had the last word. Before I left, he made a point of telling me that I had been replaced by Anna Ford, a young researcher and journalist. She was good-looking, intelligent and was applying for a job with the BBC, but she needed security clearance as she had been married to a communist. I imagined that Victor and she would get on well.

The parting with Martin was perfunctory, with feelings deliberately kept at bay. Neither of us wanted to dwell on the reasons that had led to this. Martin said that he would visit us soon, but he had to organise his own move first. He also mentioned that he had started seeing an actress called Susie Blake, confirming it was time for me to go.

It was dusk and raining hard when the children and I drove off. Shortly after I reached the motorway, the car headlights went out and the windscreen wipers stopped working. The road was busy with rush-hour traffic and, being unable to see where I was going, I swerved onto the hard shoulder. As I did so, I noticed a car pull up behind me. A man got out and came over.

'Are you in trouble?' he asked.

'Everything's gone – lights, wipers, the lot.'

'It's probably a fuse, maybe more than one. If you have any spares, I'll change them.' Without more ado, he found the fuses and fixed the problem. I asked what made him stop.

'I saw your lights go out... thought you might need help.'

I thanked him and went on my way. But the incident reminded me of the importance of trust and that help can turn up in unexpected ways.

After staying overnight with Martin's parents, I set off the following morning approaching Woman's Land along a fell road under storm-filled clouds. The landscape felt wild and untamed, and I found the prospect of beginning a new life here exhilarating. A couple of miles beyond the village of Dent, with its cobbled streets and quaint stone houses, I came to the track that led to the farmhouse. As it had already been renovated I had little to do but learn how to clear silt from the pipes that fed the water tank and take care of a few hens that the previous owner had left behind.

The local people were curious to find out about the new family that had arrived, wanting to welcome us and help Rachel settle into the village school. Within days I noticed that she had assumed a gentle Cumbrian lilt, was fitting in well and enjoying a new circle of friends. As for me, I found sanctuary in nature. Whatever the weather, I took Abi for walks by the beck, through fields of sheep and up the fell to watch the last rays of sunlight cast patterns on the other side of the valley. And when the moon was full, I sat in the garden, surprised at how light it was at midnight. Apart from the occasional hoot of an owl, all was silent and still. Dentdale was indeed a magical and sacred place.

I knew it would be a challenge finding meditation students locally, but I discovered a group of people in the Lake District who had already learned Guruji's practices. So when we heard he was planning a trip to England, we invited him to come and see us. He accepted our invitation gladly and asked if he could stay at Woman's Land with a couple of teachers who were travelling with him. After my experience of Maharishi I was wary about having a guru to stay, but those accompanying him assured me that he was the easiest of guests and there was no need to make any special arrangements.

When Guruji arrived, I was surprised to see that he was dressed in a suit and had short hair, unlike Maharishi. There was little formality, the atmosphere was relaxed and easy, and having three children of his own, Guruji enjoyed having Rachel and Abi around. Over a supper of dahl and rice, he asked me why I had come to Dentdale. I explained that since doing his practices, I had given up teaching for Maharishi, my marriage had fallen apart and I had been drawn to move far away from London.

He smiled and, in a measured voice, said, 'On the spiritual path, the more challenges we encounter the better. It's an opportunity to learn more about ourselves. Your relationship with Martin had served its purpose and needed to end... and you can now teach for me.'

I expressed my gratitude for his offer before pressing him further: 'So why do we come into this world to experience pain and suffering? What is it we need to learn?'

'To know the truth of who we are.'

'Which is what?'

'Our essence is divine. We are all children of God. But we lose our way and enter a state of forgetfulness, which is why we experience fear as soon as we are born. Suffering helps wake us up and without it we would remain in the dark. We should see it as a gift instead of a judgement as it gives us the opportunity to grow.'

I mentioned the poem I had written about the journey of the human soul and asked if we move through different timelines and dimensions.

'We're multi-dimensional beings, but only when a person transcends the limitations of this world can we experience who we truly are.'

Then he whispered the word, '*Usha... Usha*,' before telling me that this was my new name. He sounded it softly before explaining, 'It means "dawn". It's a reminder that the first rays of light appear after the darkness of the night.'

Over the next few days, Guruji travelled around the area giving talks and answering questions and, on one occasion, asked if Rachel would like to join us. She nodded enthusiastically, and when we arrived at the venue, he asked her to sit beside him. I was surprised how still she was as she listened to him. At one point, he was saying how much we were all loved, even though we do not realise it.

'You are not only loved by the Divine Mother and Divine Father, but by those who come here to teach the eternal truths. I love each one of you more than you could ever imagine... more than your father ever loved you.'

I noticed Rachel prick up her ears, aware that Martin had retreated from her life and now he rarely saw her. Guruji's comment also made me start. Here was a man whom I had only just met saying that he loved me as my father had never done. And it was true. I could feel Guruji's love – a love that was not dependent upon what I did or said or what my faults and virtues were – he loved me unconditionally for who I was.

Before he left, he asked Rachel if she would like to see a fairy.

'How?' she replied.

'Come with me,' he said, and they went off up the fell.

When they returned, Rachel looked radiant.

'Did you see one?' I asked.

'Yes, I did. We sat by a stream and he showed me how I can see a fairy whenever I want to. It was as real as I'm seeing you now.'

I had no experience of living in such a remote place in winter and so did not realise that when snow was forecast I had to leave my car on the road as the snow plough would not clear my track. After the first heavy snowfall, I was stranded for days and had to rely on a farmer bringing me supplies on a tractor. I also discovered that I had to brush away the snow from the roof slates otherwise it blew in through the rafters and left damp patches on the ceilings. When spring came, the reality of living alone up the dale with two small children became untenable as money was scarce and I could no longer afford a car. So when a three-storey cottage came up for sale in the middle of the village, I decided to move. The shop and primary school were within a hundred metres of the house, the children would have their friends close by and there was a weekly bus to the nearest market town.

The cottage was also conveniently situated between two pubs, where instructors from the nearby Cave and Fell Centre visited most evenings… and it was there that I met John. Over a pint, I asked him why he had ended up in Dentdale.

'Because I love the Dales and this is where the caves are. But I'm a chemist by training. I went to Bradford Grammar School, then Oxford, and then worked for a while before giving everything up to spend a year travelling around Spain. I always intended on coming back and getting a proper job but never got around to it. What about you? How did you end up here?'

And so our relationship began. One that enabled me to see the Dales through the eyes of someone who understood the vagaries of hill weather, cave systems, water courses and was able to navigate the fells when the mists were down. John was also considerate and caring, and offered me stability of a kind that I had not experienced before. So it was not long before footprints were seen in the snow early one morning outside my front door.

'So who was visiting you last night?' a farmer asked.

'Never you mind,' I smiled.

In the three years I had been there, my parents had only visited me once, and that was because they needed to break their journey on the way to Scotland. They were still mystified by my move to the Dales so far away from anyone I knew. But as I became more established in the dale, the more they accepted my decision and with it their concern for my welfare. So when my mother heard I was without a car, she immediately offered me the loan of hers.

'You'll have to come and fetch it, though,' she said, keen that I should visit them in Cambridge. 'We're planning on moving and we want to show you a couple of properties.'

When I arrived, my father explained that it was time they

moved to a smaller house. Then my mother told me the news that she really wanted to share.

'I've been offered a peerage. But it's not public yet so you mustn't tell anyone.'

I offered my congratulations, realising what such an honour would mean to her. She would now have a title, prestige and an opportunity to dedicate herself to the political causes that were closest to her heart – equal opportunities in education and the environment. But how, I wondered, had a Cambridge County Councillor been elevated to this status?

'Pat Llewellyn Davies put my name forward,' she explained. 'As Prime Minister, Jim Callaghan is keen on having more working peers.'

My mother had known Pat since university days and she and her husband Richard were close friends of the Rothschilds. Richard had been an Apostle and courted left-wing ideals – both he and Pat were now life peers. So I guessed that strings had been pulled which had allowed my mother to become a peer of the realm.

Whether it was the extra celebratory drink to mark the occasion or the fact that my parents and I were together again, the atmosphere was jovial and relaxed, which allowed me to broach more sensitive subjects. Prompted by Victor talking about his open marriage arrangement with Tess, I asked about his relationship with Barbara, his first wife, and why they had divorced. My mother poured herself another glass of wine before replying.

'Barbara had affairs and Victor could not cope with her infidelity. She was an extrovert, fun-loving, and enjoyed her independence.'

I noticed my mother glance at my father before continuing: 'What she really wanted was to have an affair with Dick.'

'And did you?' I asked, looking directly at him. 'You'd have been a catch for any woman.'

'No,' he said, and then added, 'but your mother would have liked me to.'

'Would you, Mum?' I asked, intrigued by where the conversation was leading.

But my father continued before she had a chance to answer: 'I never wanted affairs. I loved your mother and she alone... it was different for her.'

'In what way?' I asked.

'Your mother was gregarious. She's always enjoyed parties and socialising.'

At this point my mother disappeared into the kitchen to finish supper preparations. No doubt she thought enough had been revealed. But I sensed relief in them both that they had expressed themselves freely, knowing I would not judge or disapprove. And it was clear from the conversation that while my mother had no doubt indulged her passions, my father had remained loyal to his wife.

Over supper, I changed the subject by asking my father how he felt about my mother becoming a peer.

'I'm pleased for her, but when I retired I imagined that we would travel and spend more time together. Now it seems we'll go back to seeing each other only at weekends.'

'You can come and stay with me,' I offered. 'The house is basic but comfortable enough.'

He seemed pleased by the invitation so I decided to tell them about John, making sure I included his academic achievements, knowing that this would impress them.

'He's different from Martin, reliable and steady. We're thinking of getting married.'

'Can't you wait?' was my mother's immediate response. 'He won't be earning much.'

Social and financial status were of utmost importance to her and John had neither.

'We'll manage,' I assured her. 'I'm used to making a little money go a long way.'

It was a relief to have told them as I did not want anything to come between us again. When we finally went to bed, I felt buoyant, glad that I had been able to navigate a conversation in which my parents had confided in me and I had been truthful with them. It felt as though a new benchmark in our relationship had been set.

OLD WOUNDS

~

Inspired by Guruji's visit, I began giving talks about the benefits of meditation to the local community and managed to attract some students. John was curious about meditation but, as a scientist and rationalist, doubted its relevance to him or our future together. It was apparent that we were on different paths. His passion was to explore the outer world, while mine was to discover our inner reality. But after my marriage with Martin, I did not want anything to cloud our relationship. So on the first day of our honeymoon, while looking out over a wild Cornish sea, I told John that I was going to give up teaching as well as meditating in order to devote myself to him and our marriage. In making such a commitment, I believed I was doing everything I could to give our relationship the best chance.

'What do you mean?' he asked in astonishment. 'You don't have to do this for me.'

'I know I don't. But it's time to have a break from my past. I want to see the world through your eyes… explore the fells and see the caves you're so passionate about. I'm ready for a change.'

I did not see my gesture as a sacrifice but as a way of reinforcing our love for one another, along with embracing new adventures and possibilities. I was excited by the prospect of learning how to prusik and abseil, so I could appreciate the wonders of the underground world – hundred-metre waterfalls, stream passages, rock sculptures and pristine formations that hung from a cave roof.

The birth of Charlotte, however, put a temporary end to my caving exploits and, in the first year of her life, I began to feel adrift once again. With Rachel and Abi at school, I turned my attention to baking bread, making yoghurt, churning butter and gathering flowers and berries to make jam and wine. But despite enjoying my domestic pursuits, I could feel frustration growing within me. There was a part of me that needed an outlet, a means of self-expression. So while Charlotte was still young, I picked up my camera again and began capturing on film the landscape and people I had grown to love. As John enjoyed photography too, he helped me set up a darkroom so we could print our own black and white pictures. When people in the village found out what we were doing, they were soon knocking on the door and asking to buy prints.

So when news came that the Cave and Fell Centre was soon to close and all the instructors would be made redundant, we already had another potential source of income. Living where we did, we were in an ideal position to document in detail the life and landscape of the northern hills. Not only were we on hand to go out in all weathers and capture the landscape, but we also had developed a close connection with the farming community, and were able to photograph the underground world too. As our collection of pictures grew, a local publisher-printer offered to sponsor us while we compiled our work into a couple of books, portraying the life and landscape of the Dales and Lake District in the 1980s.

Intrigued by our foray into the publishing world, my father began visiting us more regularly, timing his stays when the sedges, orchids and bird's-eye primrose were in flower. He was the easiest of guests, appreciating whatever meals I offered him, whether it was a bowl of soup and homemade bread, or fish pie washed down with a glass of elderflower wine. He relaxed in the gentle rhythm of family life, enjoying the children and getting to know Rachel, now a teenager, whom he had always adored. When he returned from his botanical trips, he looked over our work, suggested edits and shared ideas about design and layout, before sitting by the fire and picking up his favourite Trollope novel.

I looked forward to the times when he came to stay. Without my mother, I was able to engage with him on a deeper level, aware that there were subjects he was happy to talk about and others he preferred to avoid. I wanted to find out more about his experiences in the war – what it was like floating on a mattress in the Mediterranean Sea after being torpedoed; and throwing away barrels of brandy in Alexandria to stop his sailors getting drunk; then learning about the loss of his favourite brother. But the story he was drawn to share was his struggle in going to war at all.

'I've never seen myself as a Quaker, but I've always sympathised with their policy of finding peaceful solutions rather than taking up arms. So at the beginning of World War II, I was in a state of utter confusion as to whether I should enlist or not.'

'So what made you go?' I asked.

'One day I was in my office at the press feeling wretched about it all. I knew that Hitler had to be stopped, but I believed that there must be another way of doing it rather than by force. Then I did something very unexpected. I got down on my knees and prayed. I asked for help, some guidance, and something in me changed. As I prayed, I knew that we had no option other than to bring Hitler down, and if that meant going to war, so be it. That's when I joined the navy and became a navigator.'

I could not imagine my father getting down on his knees and praying and was touched that he had shared the story. This led to another tale about a Botticelli print of *The Birth of Venus* that he had given me and now hung above the mantlepiece in our sitting room.

'That picture was in my cabin throughout the war and was my lifeline. Do you see the two winds on the left, Aura and Zephyr, blowing Venus into the shore?' he said, pointing at the picture.

'Nora looks just like Aura, so every time I looked at the painting, I thought of her, and that's what helped me through the war.'

Such times with my father were precious and I began to realise the deep love that he had for my mother, despite her volatile temperament and determination to pursue her career instead of spending time with her husband during his retirement. I observed that she never came north with him and rarely accompanied him on trips abroad, so I decided to go to London to see what her new life was like. My mother was pleased.

'I'll give you lunch at the House of Lords and you can bring Rachel too.'

Rachel was now old enough to appreciate a visit to the Houses of Parliament and she was proud of her grandmother, who had a seat in the Lords. When we arrived, we were greeted by ushers, who showed us into the central hallway where we waited for my mother to appear. She swept down the corridor with a broad smile, embraced us, before looking me up and down.

'Your hair could do with a brush, Elizabeth.'

'I've already brushed it,' I replied, not wishing to jump to her demands as a matter of course.

'Well, do it again,' she said. 'The ladies' room is over there.'

At the time I had long, wavy hair and it was difficult to make it look manicured. But I did as I was told and came out smiling, wondering if she would ever stop issuing commands. But I knew that appearances were important to her, especially when introducing the family to her colleagues. As she took us through to her office, I was struck by the complexity of the building with a maze of corridors, side rooms, offices and out-of-the-way lifts going to different floors. My mother shared an office with Pat Llewellyn Davies, who was glad to see me again after all these years and recalled the time Emma and I had played together as children. My mother then took us through to the Throne Room, explaining that this was where the Queen presided over official ceremonies and donned her robes and crown before entering the Chamber.

Then she showed us the Royal Gallery and pointed out the signed warrant for the execution of King Charles I.

'Is that really a death warrant for a King?' Rachel asked in surprise.

'It is indeed.'

My mother was an adept host, having a natural ability to make guests feel at ease while at the same time pointing out items of interest, famous politicians and ex-prime ministers. She was pleased with of her new status and wanted Rachel and me to appreciate the corridors of power and their importance and relevance in our history. As we made our way to the Peers' Dining Room, I caught sight of two familiar faces, Bob and Wanda. She was immaculately turned out in a dark blue dress and a brightly coloured scarf while Bob was wearing a suit, bow tie and, as was his custom, a carnation in his lapel. It took a moment for them to realise who we were.

'Well, well, well, my treasure,' Bob said, taking me in his arms before turning to Rachel. 'What a big girl you are and so beautiful.'

My first impression was how much Bob had aged. He was thinner and I noticed that he now had a slight tremor. I imagined that drink had finally got the better of him. It was clearly a struggle for him to make conversation, so I did not burden him with news of life in the North. Wanda took charge to save Bob the effort of remembering, or the embarrassment of forgetting. But his spark and sense of humour were still there. I guessed his visits to the House were brief, probably just to collect his attendance fee. He had left himself and Wanda little money, having spent it or given it away, and I was one of his beneficiaries. As they turned to go, I noticed Bob steadying himself on Wanda's arm and wondered if this would be the last time I saw him. So before going into the dining room, I turned to have another look at this once great man, now a shadow of his former self who, through his kindness and generosity, had changed the course of my life.

It was a while after my visit to the Lords that my mother called to say that Bob had suffered a heart attack and had passed away at Westminster Hospital. Apparently he had been living on whisky and Complan and had continued to lose weight and had joked with his nephew, Ludovic Kennedy, that euthanasia should be compulsory after a certain age. He was clearly ready to go so I did not grieve his passing, but offered up gratitude for his presence in my life and all that he had meant to me. My mother never talked about the funeral arrangements to either Teresa or me, so we never had the chance of going. Instead I wrote to Wanda to offer my condolences:

> *How well I remember the times he visited us in Cambridge, the endless lunches at Eaton Square, the gifts and treats he gave me. There was always a feeling of lightness, gaiety and fun when Bob was around. He wasn't my godfather, but it felt as though he was – not just a godfather but a fairy godfather too. When I was eight years old and I broke my arm, he said I could have anything I wanted. I asked for a camera and now I am a photographer. What an inspiration he was, what a difference he made to my life. I loved him dearly.*

Moved by what I had written, Wanda asked if my words could be used in a biography that Robert Rhodes James was writing about Bob. In the book I was referred to as 'one of his favourite children' and was touched that he regarded me as such. It was not until a while later that I found out that Wanda had honoured Bob's wish to be buried at sea. She had taken his ashes to Aberdeenshire, the constituency that he had served and loved, boarded a drifter called *Starlight* and headed out to sea on a wild and windy day. A flotilla of fishing boats joined them and a mile from Rattray Head, she cast his ashes into the sea along with numerous wreaths from others who were present. When thanking those who had come, she said that the farmers and North Sea fishermen had always been close to Bob's heart. And with that I felt at peace, knowing that he had come home at last.

As John and I now had transport in the form of a VW campervan, I made regular trips to Cambridge so that my mother could see the children. But John only came when there was a family gathering and, if there was no space in the house, we stayed at the Rothschilds'. As family get-togethers always involved a lengthy dinner, we arrived at Herschel Road late at night. The caretaker showed us in and as all was quiet, we made our way to the guest room. Everything was familiar – the bedding, towels, bathroom and even the soap – it was like going back to my past. John appreciated the comfort of the room, scanned through the books and was pleased to find one on bats. He leafed through it, marvelling at the exquisite illustrations and descriptions of these extraordinary flying mammals.

'They've probably forgotten they've even got this book,' he said wryly.

'You can't say that.' I smiled, sinking into bed, but thought he was probably right.

As we went downstairs for breakfast the following morning, I felt slightly apprehensive. As neither Victor nor Tess had met John before, I wondered what they would make of him. I pushed open the dining room door and saw Victor sitting one side of the table and Tess on the other. Newspapers were strewn everywhere. Seemingly engrossed in what they were reading, they said nothing to welcome us. I was bemused but not surprised, as I was accustomed to unpredictable behaviour when staying with the Rothschilds. After a while, Tess asked if we would like a paper, before gesturing to the hotplate to help ourselves to breakfast. Victor remained silent. I knew that he was only there to meet John, curious to see the man that I had chosen as my second husband. But clearly Victor had no intention of interacting with him. It was John who paved the way by commenting on the book on bats that he seen the night before. At once Victor put down his paper, turned towards me and asked, 'How do bats navigate, Biff?'

'Sonar,' I replied immediately, amused that I was back to my childhood name and he was up to his old tricks.

He was taken aback, maybe surprised that I had the correct answer, but I was married to a caver so I knew about bats. Seemingly irritated at not catching me out, Victor helped himself to another sausage before burying his head in the newspaper again. But the incident generated conversation with Tess, who asked about the family and how my mother was faring at the House of Lords. When we left, I asked John what he thought of Victor.

'I hated the way he treated you, trying to make you look stupid when you're not.'

'It's about control,' I explained. 'He always has to be in charge and he disliked me being there with you. I suspected he might behave like that, but oddly enough I didn't mind it this time.'

'Well, I didn't like it… nor him,' John retorted, and I sympathised with how he felt.

But for me the exchange reflected how I had changed as I was no longer affected by either Victor's attitude or his questions. I imagined that Victor had been surprised by my choice of husbands, and it was true: John and I were very different. Discussions about the meaning of life and our purpose on Earth always ended abruptly. At times there seemed an unbridgeable gulf between John's pragmatic view of the world and mine. When this happened, I always brought the conversation back to the meaning of love.

'You can't deny it exists, but you can't prove it either,' I challenged. 'Love is an energy that connects people… it flows between us. It can't be broken down into subatomic particles and quarks, but nevertheless we experience it as a tangible, powerful force.'

Temporarily this silenced him. But I was beginning to wonder whether I had taken the right decision by making our marriage the priority instead of my own inner search for truth. It had been my own choice to put my spiritual aspirations on hold, but I sensed it was now time for a change. I expressed how I felt to John.

'I feel parched… empty inside. I no longer meditate nor teach others the practice that changed my life. I feel as though I've lost my way.'

'What do you want to do?' he asked, with tenderness in his voice.

'I don't know, but I need some guidance, some inspiration to help me get back on my path.'

Over the past few months, Guruji kept coming to mind, the teacher and guide that I trusted the most. I had heard that he was still running courses, so I began making enquiries and was told that he had just completed a tour of America and Europe and was now back in South Africa. When he found out that I was asking about him, he suggested I phone him in Cape Town. I was moved by his response: 'I've been calling for you, Usha. Where have you been all these years? You've been in the wilderness, going round and round in circles. I'm running a retreat for some of the teachers in Cyprus. Why don't you come? It would do you good.'

As our first book of photographs had just been published, we had some spare money and John encouraged me to go. However, I was not prepared for what I was about to experience. Whether it was the practices, transmissions or wisdom that Guruji imparted throughout the day and night I was not sure, but the experience knocked me sideways. Intense feelings ranged from the pain of abandonment, long-held hurt, to a need to be valued and cherished, reminding me of how I felt as a child. At other times I had bolts of energy shooting through me and then a sense of connectedness when I felt at one with everyone and everything around me. As an attempt to ground myself, I went to a nearby cove and swam vigorously in a cold February sea, or walked through the narrow streets of Limassol, savouring the smell of oils, herbs and freshly baked bread.

I returned home feeling different, as though I had been shown aspects of myself that were now ready to be healed. After that, whenever Guruji came to England, I made sure that I attended his retreats. During these times, he never let me out of his sight and continually expressed his love and appreciation of me. He said that he wanted me to learn his art, how he inspired his students, mirrored back their insecurities and gave them practices that would bring into alignment their conflicted energies. And the more time we spent together, the more I could feel his love permeating every part of me, and I felt wanted, valued and understood at the deepest level of my being.

But the last time he visited England, my experience was totally different. He seemed to have forgotten who I was. It was as though he had never met me. I was bewildered, unable to understand how he could treat me in such a heartless way. As I became increasingly engulfed by feelings of hurt and rejection, I recognised that all my old wounds were still active. Occasionally I caught Guruji looking at me, through me, to see how far I had progressed on my journey and how I was coping with what was happening now. He knew that all my life I had looked to another for love – my father, mother, Martin, John and finally my guru – and now he wanted to free me from that need. So as the days went by and I nursed my hurt, I began to understand that all he desired was for me to experience the infinite love that resides within us all and is not dependent upon anyone.

It was only a few weeks later that Guruji passed away. When I heard the news it was as though his essence, his spirit, had suddenly landed in my heart. Freed from the constraints of his body, I felt closer to him than I had ever been. By turning me away, he had freed me from the need for his love. So I lit a candle and offered up gratitude to Guruji and all those great teachers who come to Earth to help humanity awaken from the dream of separation.

Unanswered Questions

My mother was diligent in keeping me up to date with Cambridge news and at times she surprised me, such as the time she told me that rumours were circulating about Victor's possible involvement with the Cambridge spy ring. The idea was viewed with incredulity by my parents' friends, most of whom dismissed it as an impossibility. But in 1979 it was confirmed that Anthony Blunt, a respected art historian with royal connections, was the fourth member of the spy ring. Like Guy Burgess, Victor and Tess had known him from university days and they had been close friends ever since. I remembered seeing him at Merton Hall as a child. So I asked my mother how the Rothschilds had taken the news that another of their close friends had been exposed as a spy.

'They can't believe it. They're terribly upset by the whole affair.'

I was puzzled by her comment. Victor was highly perceptive and discerning, so how could someone he knew so well have deceived him for almost fifty years? My experience of Victor was that he could see through anyone.

A few years later, events had moved on. Not only had four members of the Cambridge spy ring now been officially exposed, but it was also known there was a fifth man who had masterminded the ring's operations both during and after the war. The question now being asked was whether this was Victor. As MI5 and MI6 pursued different lines of enquiry, Victor's spirits sank ever lower. I knew nothing of spy rings or espionage but, if there was a fifth man, it could easily be him. Not only did he have close association with others in the spy ring, but during the war he had leased his London house to Anthony Blunt and Guy Burgess. Pat Llewellyn Davies and Tess had also lived there, and Victor was a frequent visitor. Like Kim Philby and Don Maclean, the other two spies, they all embraced left-wing Marxist ideologies.

It was not difficult imagining Victor as the controller of one of the most successful operations in the history of espionage. He had an IQ that put him in the genius category, and was a discerning and innovative scientist. He also had access to Intelligence agencies as well as inside knowledge of the banking world and government. This meant that he was placed in an ideal position to access information and pass it on to the KGB, or anyone else he chose to inform. Not only this, Victor also cultivated friendships with prime ministers and heads of state, knowing it was a way of procuring information and being an influencer. As I had experienced, none of us really knew who the real Victor was. He wore different masks according to the company he kept. One moment he could be witty and charming, and the next, ruthless and unyielding. He was an enigma and I doubted that he revealed the truth of himself to anyone… not even Tess.

As pressure increased within political circles for the fifth man to be identified, my parents became increasingly concerned. As the list of possible suspects was narrowed down, the strain took its toll not only on Victor but also Tess, the family and friends. Dinner and drinks parties at Herschel Road became a distant memory as Victor's mental health deteriorated.

My mother talked to me about it openly, curious to know my thoughts.

'If there was a fifth man, it might well be Victor,' I mused. 'I doubt he would have any conscience about passing on intelligence to the Russians or anyone else if he thought it would further his cause.'

My mother seemed relieved by my honesty, glad that she could talk to me without fear of judgment or blame. She neither sprang to Victor's defence nor ruled out the possibility of him having an involvement with the spy ring. After all, she had witnessed first hand the close friendship Victor and Tess had with the other spies. Indeed, she had socialised with them too. I mentioned that I doubted Victor would have any regrets about what he may or may not have done. For him, the greatest humiliation would be being found out. So perhaps it was this that triggered his depression?

In the midst of the undercurrent of speculation and suspicion, Victor expressed a wish to see me again. I was pleased as I wanted to erase the memory of my last visit to Herschel Road. My father booked a table for dinner at the Garrick Club for Victor, Tess, my parents and me, and said how much they looked forward to the occasion. When I arrived, Victor and Tess were already waiting in the foyer. My first impression of Victor was how much he had aged. He now walked with a stick, had a slight stoop and his eyes had a look of resignation… or perhaps it was sadness? His receding hair emphasised his large forehead and his neck had thickened, giving him more of the bull-like appearance characteristic of his Rothschild ancestors. As we went upstairs to the dining room, I took his arm and told him how glad I was to see him again. At the table, he motioned me to sit next to him saying he wanted to talk to me. I could see relief on Tess's face that some of his old spark had returned. My father consulted Victor about what wine to order, while I looked through the menu and chose pheasant.

Victor commented, 'So you're eating meat again.'

'Fish and fowl, that's all. I was lacking energy and apparently trace elements too, so the doctor advised me to eat more protein.'

'I'm glad you're looking after yourself.' Victor smiled.

I was touched that despite his own concerns, he still cared for my welfare. During dinner, there was a feeling of lightness and gaiety around the table, as we fondly remembered times from the past. But it was not long before we separated into two groups, Tess in conversation with my parents, while I talked to Victor. He asked what I was doing, why I had escaped to the North and what was keeping me there. I talked about the landscape, open fells, lush green dales, quaint villages and the down-to-earth nature of the people.

'There's no pretence,' I said. 'I know where I stand with them. I feel I belong in the North and I never felt that about Cambridge. Remember, the Lakes' poets and Brontës found inspiration from the wildness of the northern landscape too.'

'Are you still writing?' he asked.

'A little… I'm more of a photographer now, documenting the life of hill farmers. At the moment we're working on a book called *Hill Shepherd* that's due out next year.'

'I think you could do better than that,' Victor said with a slightly mischievous smile. 'You were once a revolutionary with visionary ideas.'

I laughed, remembering the poems that I had shared with him. 'Maybe in the future I'll rediscover that part of myself. I hope so. John's passion is the outdoor world, so for the last few years I've been following him. But I'm re-evaluating things now. I need to start asking questions again, so thanks for reminding me of the person I once was.'

It was refreshing to have an open, honest conversation with Victor again. If we had been alone together I would have asked him about spies and spy rings, but it neither seemed the time nor the place. In that moment I just appreciated all he done for me, realising that when I was younger he had been the only person who was prepared to listen and find out about me.

At the end of the evening, we took a taxi together before going our separate ways. Victor sat next to me and at one point put his hand on my knee, squeezed it, and looking at me said, 'I miss you.'

So I placed my hand on top of his. 'I miss you too and our conversations. I'll never forget the times we spent together, or this evening.'

I knew that the others were listening, but there was a feeling of relief that Victor's spirits were lifted and he was back to his old self... for a while at least. As I accompanied my parents on the train back to Cambridge, they said they had not seen Victor in such good form for years.

I doubted that I would ever see him again. As with Bob, a brief encounter in London, a parting and subsequently another chapter in my life closed. Considering Victor's lifelong habit of smoking and his enjoyment of alcohol, it was remarkable that he lived as long as he did. He was with Tess watching television at St James's Place when he had a fatal heart attack. The funeral was private, but Tess asked if I would accompany my parents to the Memorial Service.

'Where's it to be?' I asked my mother.

'At the West London Synagogue.'

'That's absurd,' I exclaimed. 'He never went to the synagogue. He wasn't a practising Jew.'

'He's a Rothschild,' my mother explained. 'It's the tradition.'

I had never been to a synagogue, so I was curious to see how the service was conducted. When we arrived, there was a queue and ahead a counter where guests were being greeted. I noticed that the men were being offered a kippah, the skull cap that was customary for Jews to wear at religious occasions. When it was our turn, my father was handed one but he declined it, saying, 'No, thank you.'

'Please, sir, it is the custom,' the attendant said politely.

'I would prefer not,' my father insisted.

Embarrassed by the exchange and aware that others behind were listening, I wondered why he could not forego his principles for this one occasion. As the queue was building up, the attendant said, with more urgency in his voice, 'Please, sir, it is the wish of the family. They would appreciate you wearing one.'

Irritated, my father took it and reluctantly placed it on his head, but I felt uncomfortable about the exchange. It was a side of my father I rarely saw but my mother occasionally spoke of – an intolerance and impatience in him that could suddenly erupt.

As I went into the synagogue, I was impressed by the opulence of the building and noticed that screens had been placed discreetly so that parts of the ceremony could take place in private. As we waited, my parents pointed out politicians, academics and other dignitaries as they arrived. Among them was William Waldegrave, who was giving one of the addresses and I recalled him being a protege of Victor's. Then I caught sight of Emma with her sister Tory, coming in with Tess. It was the first time I had seen Emma since we had skied together when we were twelve years old. How well I remembered her distinctive bone structure and striking appearance. But now there were wisps of grey in her shoulder-length hair. The person, however, who we were all waiting for was Prime Minister Margaret Thatcher, as her appearance held a particular significance. My parents had explained that if she came it would testify to Victor's innocence – and if not, it would indicate the Government believed that he had been the fifth man in the spy ring.

I waited expectantly and was at the point of giving up, when suddenly I saw the Prime Minister walk in, brusquely accompanied by two aides. She was smaller and slighter than I expected and gave the impression that she was irritated by her afternoon's duty. Indeed, her attendance seemed like an empty gesture, signifying neither Victor's guilt nor innocence. As I listened to the eulogies interspersed with pieces of music that included a short piece by Art Tatum, I wondered what Victor would have made of the occasion. I imagined him watching from above, having the last laugh. All this pomp and ceremony in honour of a man who may have been one of the most notorious traitors of the century.

When the dust had settled, my mother began making plans to celebrate my father's eightieth birthday. Before my grandmother died, she had bequeathed the Cornish house to him and he had since passed it on to my sister, so this was where he wanted the celebration to be. It transpired, however, that because my nieces and nephews had been invited there was no room for me. I presumed my father would ask why I was not going, but there was no word from him. I was saddened but not surprised and tried to brush it off.

Instead my mother suggested that Teresa, her husband Tony, John and myself have dinner at the Garrick Club. With memories of the evening with Victor and Tess in mind, I thought this might be an opportunity to connect more closely with my father. I had always believed that I had inherited my interest in spirituality from him as he was descended from a long line of bishops and clerics. So as a means of reaching out, I took him one of my favourite books called *The Enlightened Heart*, which had quotes from his favourite poets, Dante, Shakespeare and others. At the end of the meal I handed it to him, saying that I thought he might like it, but I noticed the there was a reluctance on his part to take it. He leafed through it quickly, before passing it back, saying in a curt voice, 'I don't like that sort of thing.'

I felt crushed, as though I had done something terribly wrong. How different from the evening I had enjoyed with the Rothschilds. For weeks afterwards I reprimanded myself for making such an unnecessary blunder. Far from establishing mutual ground between us, it seemed my gesture had driven us further apart.

So it was a relief when later in the year, he asked to come and stay. As soon as he arrived he relaxed, but appeared frailer so I made sure that I knew where he was going on his botanical expeditions. On the second day, he returned with a limp and admitted that he had slipped and fallen while poking around in a wood. I had heard stories about people coming to grief in remote places and dying either of their injury or hypothermia, so I raised the subject with him.

'Dad, I think you should take a hip flask when you go botanising. If anything happens, whisky will dull the pain and take you off quickly if that's how you're destined to go.'

He laughed, amused by the idea, so I clocked up a flask as a potential Christmas present. But after that incident, he only went on short trips, so he seemed to have heeded my advice. He also assured me that when travelling abroad he now always went with a group or a friend.

'For example next year, I'm going to Corsica with the Royal Botanical Society. I've always wanted to go, but last time the trip was cancelled so I hope nothing intervenes this time.'

'Make sure you stay well and fit then,' I encouraged.

Before travelling to Corsica, my parents asked if they could come and spend a few days in Dent. I was surprised as it was too early in the year for flowers. So I decided to give them a relaxing holiday, cooking their favourite dishes, going on gentle walks by the river and visiting the places that they loved. When they arrived, however, my father had a swollen ankle, which was a worry as he was due to travel in three weeks' time. I suggested him seeing a doctor.

'I don't think that will be necessary,' my father said, not wanting a fuss.

For most of his adult life, he had suffered from duodenal ulcers and also had nerve damage in the lower part of his legs as a result of injuries from the war. But there was a tradition of stoicism within that generation and I rarely heard either of my parents complain about pain or physical discomfort. However, I knew that a swollen ankle might be indicative of heart problems.

'I can make you an appointment in a couple of minutes,' I said persuasively. 'The doctor holds a surgery in the Methodist Hall and it's only a short walk away.'

So with encouragement from my mother, he agreed to have his ankle checked. As we walked along the street, I wanted to take his arm as I had done with Victor, but I felt shy as physical closeness had never been a part of our relationship. Instead, I humoured him with village gossip as I could tell he was concerned.

The doctor invited me in so I could hear what she had to say. As expected she diagnosed oedema and told my father to keep his leg up as much as possible before his trip abroad. She also advised him to have a thorough examination as soon as he got back to Cambridge. When we returned to the cottage, I rearranged the furniture to make it easy for him to keep his leg up and, with no imperatives, we had plenty of time to talk. So I took the opportunity of asking a question that had long been on my mind.

'Tell me, when I was at boarding school, did you know that I had been relegated to the B stream when I had done so well in my exams?'

There was a look of bewilderment on my father's face, but my mother admitted that she had a vague memory of this happening.

I continued: 'I just wondered why you never asked about it.'

'I never thought to,' my mother said. 'We left those decisions to the teachers... after all, they were the ones with the expertise.'

'What about you, Dad?' I persisted.

He put his hand on his chin and looked thoughtful. 'I don't think I knew anything about it.'

'Dad,' I exclaimed, 'it was a major event in my childhood. That's why I gave up studying and left school as soon as I could.'

I laughed off the conversation, but for me it was a break-through. Through an honest exchange, truthfulness had prevailed and I felt closer to him at last. It was apparent that by sending me away to school, neither of them had felt any need to take any meaningful interest in me or my education. I then steered the conversation to more uplifting topics, such as the time my parents took me to Tuscany at the age of fifteen to see churches and art galleries and I became tipsy after drinking some Orvieto wine. And the holiday we had in Scotland with Abi and Charlotte, when we stayed in a castle and went swimming in mountain pools. Spending time with them felt nurturing and I was sad to see them go. I settled my father in the back of the car, propped his leg up on a cushion and reminded him to look after himself when he was back in Cambridge. Then I hugged my mother, saying quietly, 'Take care of him. I don't think he's well.'

She nodded and I could detect concern in her face. As she got into the car, I blew a kiss and called out to my father, 'Enjoy Corsica.'

And they drove off down the dale.

FAREWELLS

~

A few days before my father was due to fly to Corsica, my mother said that he had complained of chest pains while packing. She was not sure what to do, so I told her to call the doctor at once. That evening a locum came to see him and, after reading my father's notes, she said it was probably his duodenal ulcers playing up owing to anxiety about his imminent trip abroad. I wondered if my mother had told her about his oedema and explained that the pains were in his chest and not his abdomen. But I knew how much my father wanted to go to Corsica. The day before his flight, my mother mentioned that he still was not himself and expressed relief that he was going with people he knew.

It was only a couple of days later that I had a call from a representative from a medical insurance company.

'There's nothing to worry about, but your father's had a mild heart attack and he's been taken to hospital in Ajaccio.'

I presumed that my father had given the insurance company my number as a precaution when going on expeditions in the Dales. I asked if my mother knew.

'That's the problem, we can't locate her. Do you know where she is?'

I remembered that she was away on parliamentary duties but

assured him that I would track her down. When I told her the news, she was at a loss for words. I guessed she felt responsible for having let him go. Then quickly she began making plans, saying she would get the first flight to Ajaccio and ask my brother Nic, who was in England at the time, to follow on as soon as possible. Meanwhile, I kept abreast of events through the insurance representative, who assured me they would fly my father home as soon as he was well enough.

'Will he be able to get travel insurance again?' I asked, concerned for his future.

'That may be difficult,' he replied.

I knew my father would resent having his freedom curtailed by rules and regulations. I also suspected that the chest pains he had in England were indicative of a possible heart attack, which would make this his second... and I had heard a third can often prove fatal. So I sent him a card wishing him a speedy recovery but, as I was on the point of writing the words, 'I love you', my pen faltered. After my experience at the Garrick, I did not want him to think me sentimental or trite, yet I wanted to express my true feelings for him. So finally I summoned up courage and wrote the words, and as I did, I welled up with tears and my heart went out to him.

When my mother arrived in Corsica, she called to say how pleased he was that she had come, even though she was only allowed to visit him once a day. Apparently he was comfortable but was finding it difficult to read or focus on anything for long. But two days later when she arrived at the hospital, she was asked to wait outside his room. Through the door she could see a huddle of doctors and nurses working feverishly around his bed and knew they were trying to resuscitate him. After a while a doctor appeared, took her hand and said how sorry he was, but my father had suffered another major heart attack and there was nothing they could do to save him. He then asked her to wait while they prepare the body.

'When I was allowed in,' she said, 'I was surprised to see they had put a bandage around his head. It looked strange at first. I suppose it was to stop his jaw from dropping. It's a Catholic country so they do things differently. But his skin was smooth and he looked so young and handsome... like when we first met...'

Then her voice broke and after a quick goodbye, she put down the phone.

As my father's body had to be brought back from Corsica and my brother Sebastian was in Canada, it was three weeks before the funeral could take place. My mother was in charge of the arrangements, which she managed with her customary flair for organisation.

'I want Nic and Sebastian to do the readings and not the girls,' she said adamantly.

Amused at the way she still referred to us as 'girls', I was relieved not to have this responsibility, but I did offer my help with the flowers. So with Abi and Charlotte, now seventeen and twelve years old, we went to see Faith Raven, a botanical friend of my father's, and together we picked foliage and flowers and created three beautiful and extravagant arrangements. During the service I became mesmerised by the sight of the coffin as it looked like a wild garden – vibrant, colourful and alive. And to the sound of my father's favourite Schubert Impromptu, I allowed the tears flow. It was like a washing through, letting go of someone whom I had never really known but over the years had grown to love and respect. The only member of the family who was missing was Rachel, the granddaughter whom my father thought of as a daughter. When she was old enough, she had gone travelling and, while working on a kibbutz by the Sea of Galilee, had met Eduardo, an Argentinian, and since they had married and were living in Buenos Aires.

Tess suggested we use the drawing room at Herschel Road for family and friends to gather after the service. Again the close circle of Cambridge friends came together – Alan and Marni Hodgkin,

Noel Annan and his wife Gabriele, Dadie, who had inspired me to go into the theatre... but Victor and Dick were missing. Tess retreated to a chair and beckoned me over and, after catching up on news, we soon began talking about the past.

'I'll always remember those skiing holidays in Wengen... my time in Banyuls and Barbados too. They were key moments of my childhood.'

Tess's eyes lit up as the years rolled back and we recalled stories from that time. She was different without Victor, more relaxed, and her facial twitch had gone. I remembered Dadie once describing her as a chameleon, saying that if she outlived Victor she would either find a new life for herself or become like an empty shell. Without the dynamo of Victor driving her, I suspected that the latter was true. But she talked enthusiastically about visits to Rushbrooke to see Amschel and her grandchildren, television programmes she enjoyed and trying her luck on the lottery. I smiled to myself, amused at how someone who belonged to one of the richest families in the world had taken up gambling. As I mingled with the other guests, I noticed Noel Annan's face was severely bruised on one side.

John joined me and joked, 'Been in a fight with Mike Tyson then?'

'Yes,' Noel replied, 'and you should have seen how he ended up.'

I remembered how much I enjoyed his company as a child. When he came to visit, his light-hearted manner ensured that I was never left feeling inadequate.

My siblings and I spent the evening with my mother at home. It was a time of reflection, and tears came when she described the last time she had seen my father and how youthful he looked. I had never seen her cry before and was pleased that she was giving way to emotion at last. There was laughter too when she told us the story of the undertaker in Corsica asking how she wanted my father dressed and she replied, 'In nothing.' When he looked at her questioningly, she added, 'Well, maybe a drape.'

As we read through the multitude of cards with eulogies about my father, my mother suddenly looked up and said, 'Why doesn't anyone mention how impatient he was? He had his flaws.'

Her remark reminded me of the importance of honesty when someone has passed on. After all, it is our faults as well as our strengths that makes us who we are. So I wondered what I would say about my mother when she had passed on. She then spoke hesitantly about her guilt in encouraging my father to go to Corsica, knowing that he was not well.

'I had a busy week at the House of Lords so it suited me that he was away... but I could have stopped him going.'

I tried to console her: 'Mum, if you have a heart attack, we'll put you on a couple of air flights to make sure you go quickly. Dad wouldn't have wanted to linger on, not well enough to go on expeditions and travel abroad again.'

And Sebastian added, 'The doctor confirmed that the locum had misdiagnosed and said the same. He would have been relieved to go the way he did.'

When I arrived home, I saw the card I had sent to my father in Corsica lying on the doormat. On it was written: *Return undelivered.* Feelings of regret swept through me, knowing that he had never received it and had been oblivious to my final attempt to tell him that I loved him. Despite all the times we had spent together and the experiences we had shared, I had never been able to express how I felt. And when eventually I found the courage to do so, it was too late. Yet the story reflected the truth of our relationship. There had always been something missing. I had sought love and understanding from him, and for some reason my father never felt able to give it. I did not blame him or judge myself, but I recognised that apart from a few treasured moments, there had been an unbridgeable gulf between us.

However, I did have a chance to record a poignant memory of him. My mother suggested publishing a book about my father and asking friends and colleagues to contribute, and I wrote the final piece. In it I shared stories about the times he had stayed with us in the Dales, the help he had given us with our books and quoted a sentence from one of them:

As the sun sinks lower in the sky and the slanting light picks out each petal and leaf, the ethereal nature of the landscape is imprinted upon my mind, as will always be the memory of my father.

We had the book launch at Herschel Road, but Tess appeared withdrawn. I heard later that she was facing challenges of her own. Roland Perry had recently published a book titled *The Fifth Man* and had named Victor as the mastermind behind the Cambridge spy ring. After extensive research and interviews with key people of that time, Perry had concluded that Victor was the only person who had the skills, expertise and access to different sources of intelligence to run the operation without arousing suspicion. The revelation did not surprise me, although I never bought the book. But its publication sent reverberations through the Rothschild family and took its toll on Tess's mental and physical health.

In the following months, her health deteriorated, and as the family became increasingly concerned about her, the news came that she had finally she passed on. Another funeral, this time at St Nicolas's Church in Rushbrooke, to which my mother and I were invited. The sun was shining and there was not a cloud in the sky as we drove through the Suffolk countryside and fields of purple lavender. When we arrived, we strolled around Rushbrooke village and I was reminded of its uniform white houses that Richard Llewellyn Davies had designed for Victor. As we went into the church, I was surprised by the arrangement of the dark wooden pews that faced inward like choir stalls, instead of to the east and the altar. But I found it difficult to focus on the service as memories of Tess kept flooding back and the feeling of calm that she emanated no matter what was happening around her. Images of her came and went – drinking iced coffee on the red and white check loungers on the verandah, reading the paper in the drawing room and entertaining guests, always interested to hear their news. After the service we went to the main house for lunch and my mother noticed that we were almost the only people there who were not Rothschilds or de Rothschilds.

Emma greeted us with a radiant smile. I then went through to the dining room, where the table was laid with a spread of cold meats, patés, cheeses and an array of unusual salads. I heard mention that the wine was the finest from the Rothschild cellars and I had a glass of Sancerre. As I helped myself to lunch, Amschel came across to welcome me. Victor had passed the Rushbrooke estate on to him, so he now ran the farm. It was the first time I had seen him since he was a young boy.

'I remember you when you were half my size,' I smiled.

Amschel laughed. 'It must be strange being back here after all these years.'

'Yes, but it still feels the same,' I said, looking around at the same decor and furniture.

'Yes, things are pretty much as they were.'

'I hear you race cars and fly aeroplanes now,' I said, recalling that he had numerous successes under his belt.

'Less so now that I'm working for the Bank.'

'Are you enjoying it?'

'To my surprise, yes.'

But before we could say more, he was ushered away to talk to another guest.

It was true. Nothing really had changed. Even the William Morris wallpaper in the downstairs cloakroom and the bench-like wooden lavatory seat with a pull-up handle on one side. As I walked through to the drawing room I saw Sarah, Victor's eldest daughter.

'Biff,' she exclaimed, 'how good to see you again. It's been years.'

Dick with Rachel in Cambridge – 1970

Nora – 1970

John, Eliza and Charlotte – 1980

Eliza on a photo shoot – 1988

Rachel, Abi and Charlotte – 1983

Rachel, Abi and Charlotte – 1990

Guruji and Eliza – 1987

David and Eliza's wedding in Seychelles – 2007

The Meditation Centre, Dent

David and Eliza in Bethany, Palestine – 2014

Four generations – Granny, Nora, Eliza and Rachel – 1970

Four generations – Eliza, Rachel, Ayelen and Shara – 2020

Book launch of The Mystery of Martha *with Teresa and Eliza in front row – 2019*

Eliza, Tim, Charlotte, Jason, Rachel and Shara visiting Aberdeenshire

Eliza at Ellerbank

Sunrise in Dentdale

'It has indeed,' I agreed. 'I'm still trying to take everything in.'

'I can't believe how little has changed,' she said, making the same observation as me. 'Even the family photographs are the same.'

But I noticed that there was a change. The feeling in the drawing room felt heavy and oppressive, something I had never experienced as a child. Whether it was because it was filled with Rothschilds dressed in dark grey or black I was not sure, but the atmosphere was tense – one of privacy and earnest conversation. It was difficult to detect any feeling of lightness or joy, a quality that Tess always brought to her home. I noticed Jacob, Victor's eldest son, so went over to talk to him. I knew that he and his father had fallen out a long time ago, which resulted in him leaving the Rothschild Bank and branching out on his own. It was now said that he was one of the richest people in the world. Like Sarah, he addressed me as 'Biff', so I mentioned that I was now 'Eliza'.

'But names stick,' he said.

'As do memories of people and places,' I replied.

'Such as what?' he asked.

'You racing on motor bikes with my brother Nic and him falling off. I still remember seeing the hole in his side.'

Jacob laughed, amused by the pranks they got up to when they were eighteen years old. He then asked me what I was doing, so I told him about my photography, writing and that our latest book celebrated the different ways in which people found spiritual fulfilment today. He seemed interested and began asking me about it, but then he too was drawn away by another guest.

On our way home to Cambridge, my mother talked about Anita, Amschel's wife. She explained that she was from the Guinness family and very wealthy in her own right.

'As I've always said, money marries money,' she concluded.

And she went on to tell me how much Amschel enjoyed running the Rushbrooke estate, racing cars and shooting partridge, and how pleased Victor was when he finally decided to join the Bank. Apparently he had risen through the ranks quickly, was now Executive Chairman and one day was destined to take over from his cousin, Evelyn de Rothschild.

So when only five weeks later, I heard about Amschel's death, I was deeply shocked. I was told that it was suicide, but the circumstances seemed strange. He had been in Paris for a business meeting, staying at the Hôtel de Bristol and was found in his bathroom with one end of his bathrobe cord around his neck and the other attached to a radiator.

It was not until two years, after Tess and Amschel's deaths, that I had another encounter with the Rothschilds. Emma's husband Amartya Sen, an Indian economist, had recently been appointed Master of Trinity College and had been awarded the Nobel Prize for his work in alleviating world poverty. To celebrate the occasion, Emma invited my mother and me for a drink to toast her husband's success and a bottle of champagne was brought from the college cellars. When we had raised our glasses, we talked about Amartya's new role, what it was like living in the Master's Lodge and the privileges that went with the post. The conversation then moved on to inheritance and money. My mother had always been very fond of Emma and Tory and occasionally had expressed concern about the Jewish custom of leaving the family inheritance to the sons rather than the daughters. So as Amschel had been left the lion's share of Victor's estate, it had now all gone to his wife Anita, leaving Emma and Tory with little.

'I don't know why Tess didn't change her will after Victor died,' my mother conjectured. 'She could have made sure that you and Tory had enough.'

I was amused by my mother's naivety. I guessed that changing a Rothschild will would not have been allowed. But spending time with Emma reminded me of her openness and sense of humour, and I was delighted that she had found happiness with Amartya as her love life had been chequered. During the eighties she had moved to Sweden to serve as an advisor to Olof Palme, the Swedish prime minister, and subsequently became romantically involved with him. Their affair was no secret, but tragedy occurred in 1986 when Palme went to the cinema with his wife and on their way back home was shot dead at point-blank range. No one understood why it took so long for the police to arrive, for Palme to be identified and for all exits out of the capital city to be closed to prevent the killer from escaping. And despite an extensive investigation that lasted for years, neither a motive nor the assassin were ever found.

So I mused as to why three unexpected deaths had occurred within one generation of Rothschilds – the murder of Miranda's husband, the assassination of Emma's lover and the alleged suicide of Amschel? Certainly the detectives who arrived at his hotel were in no doubt that they were at a murder scene. All it took was one of them to give a sharp tug on the radiator for it to come away from the wall, so Amschel could not have used it to strangle himself. There was no suicide note either, nor any reason for Amschel to take his life. Yet President Chirac put an immediate stop to any inquiry and Rupert Murdoch instructed all his media outlets to quash the story or say it was a heart attack and relegate it to the back page. It was not until a while later that I found a quote from one of Amschel's colleagues:

> *Far from being troubled, he was a rising star in the bank and relishing his success. I don't believe for a moment that he killed himself. I'm sure there's much more to the story.*

And I was in little doubt that there was.

A New Direction

~

Since my father's death, I noticed that my mother liked to honour his memory by making the annual trip to the opera at Glyndebourne, visiting his botanical friends in Scotland, listening to his favourite Bach cantatas or a Wagner overture. Similarly, she began making regular visits to Dent, curious to see the limestone crags and pavements where my father had looked for flowers. On one occasion my sister came with her and mentioned that while they were staying, there was a programme about Bob on the television. I asked what it was about and she said that my mother might find it challenging, as it revealed the truth about Bob's sexuality and friendship with the Kray twins. I expressed concern about her watching it. If Bob had been her lover, she would want to keep her memory of him as it was, rather than discover sides to his character of which she may have been oblivious.

Since Bob had died, she had also forged a close relationship with Wanda, with whom she stayed when she was in London. The arrangement suited them both. As Bob had left Wanda little money, my mother's contributions towards her rent enabled her to continue living at Eaton Square. In return, Wanda cared for my mother, made her a meal when she got back from the House of Lords, took her to exclusive shops and used her flair for style to help her buy clothes. Knowing that Wanda avoided all conversation about Bob's relationship with the Krays, I imagined my mother would do likewise. But my sister and I agreed the decision as to whether she watched it or not was hers, and she seemed up for it.

When the programme was about to start, I made the excuse of clearing away supper to avoid seeing my mother's reaction to it. I knew it was not going to portray Bob in a good light. I remembered when the *Sunday Mirror* story broke that I had doubted Bob's version at the time, as both Teresa and I had met Ronnie Kray at Eaton Square. During the television programme I went into the sitting room and, to my relief, saw my mother fast asleep. My sister commented that she had hardly seen any of the programme. But from the expression on Teresa's face, I could tell that she was shocked by what had been revealed. He was her godfather after all. And now that Bob's private life was out in the open, the full extent of his sexual proclivities was there for everyone to know.

With conflicting feelings about Bob and his past, I put the matter to one side, hoping for my mother's sake that the stories and publicity would soon die down. With the publication of our latest book *The Light Within*, John and I agreed that we were both ready for a change and he was now drawn to proof-reading. As for me, I wanted to return to teaching meditation. I realised that the gulf between us was growing but neither of us knew how to bridge it… or even if we wanted to. We had been together for twenty years, raised three children and produced six books, but he was still drawn to the outdoor world, and I wanted to discover the nature of our inner reality and who I truly am.

Rachel and Eduardo had moved from Argentina to southern Spain and now lived in a farmhouse in the Alpujarran hills. Staying with them not only gave me the chance of seeing the family but also having more honest conversations with John. I told him about my idea of setting up a meditation centre in Dentdale, where I could train people to teach and offer more insight into different approaches to spirituality.

'All paths lead to the same end,' I told him, 'so I want to remind people that there's more that unites than divides us.'

'And what about you and me? Is it the same for us?'

And his comment made me realise that concerns about our future were stirring within us both.

But the idea of Dent Meditation Centre had been conceived. In the village there was a neglected schoolroom adjoining the United Reformed Church where we kept our books. Although it was in a state of disrepair, I saw its potential as an oasis of calm and tranquillity. I imagined it as a comfortable, simply furnished room with floor cushions and a table for flowers and a candle, where anyone could find peace. So I approached the United Reform Church, who owned the building, and they agreed that if I took responsibility for renovating it I could use it for a peppercorn rent. I had no difficulty in attracting the interest of charities and benefactors, and before long the money for the restoration was flowing in. Within months, the schoolroom was transformed into an inspirational space that anyone could use for meditation or quiet reflection throughout the year.

But for the centre to have professional status, I wanted it to be a charity, which meant appointing trustees – and one of those I approached was David. He was a respected osteopath, had long experience of meditation and understood the difference between the benefits that arose from spiritual practice and those that came from personal therapy. So he had a reputation for encouraging his patients to look deeper within themselves to find the origins of their pain, realising this was where true healing began. I had experienced this when I was suffering from shoulder and neck pain.

'What are you protecting yourself from?' he asked.

'I didn't know I was,' I replied, surprised by his question.

'The muscles in your upper back are very contracted, which usually means we are shielding ourselves from hurt.'

I chose not to respond but instead asked when such patterns are first imprinted upon us.

'In infancy... or even perhaps in the womb. A foetus is bound to pick up what their mother is feeling.'

'So could I be affected by my mother's emotional state when she was carrying me?'

'Yes, it's highly likely.'

I mentioned that I had meditated for years and believed this was the best way of releasing deep-seated patterns.

'But it doesn't seem to have freed you,' he smiled. 'I'm sure it helps, but I think if we are to move beyond our conditioning, it takes more than just meditation.'

It was refreshing to hear his views about a subject that had preoccupied me for years. Guruji had talked about impressions being imprinted upon consciousness at an early age and the importance of erasing them through meditation and spiritual practice. He also said that life was our teacher and that we should regard every experience as a gift to help us see those parts of ourselves that we prefer to avoid.

As David became increasingly involved with the centre, he inspired me to probe deeper. I listened to his ideas and was surprised how easy I found it to reveal to him my innermost fears and insecurities. With him there was a connection of minds and hearts along with mutual understanding and respect. And as we grew closer, John and I drifted further apart.

No longer did I feel able to be open with John or talk about issues that were uppermost in my mind. Our photographic pursuits had allowed us to share ideas and make plans for the future, but now there was an emptiness within our relationship that seemed impossible to fill. Conversations orientated around practicalities and were all too often conducted with a veneer of politeness. The friction between us was telling on us both and I genuinely believed that he would be much happier with someone who shared his own passions and interests. It was no different for me. But in my heart I knew that this impasse would only be resolved when I found the courage to be totally truthful with him.

I knew it was not a time for hesitancy or prevarication. John's mind was centred in logic and reason and, when trying to engage with him at a deeper level, it was like confronting a steel wall. This was a case when truth had to be like a sword and strike cleanly. So from a place of calm and clarity, I told him that I wanted us to go our separate ways. As I spoke, I could feel the shockwaves go through him, but it was not my place to protect him. All I could do was express how I felt in an open and honest way. It was apparent that he already sensed the end was coming, but I knew how we all beguile ourselves. I expected his response to be one of anger or sadness, but instead it was one of disbelief.

I did my best to reassure him: 'Separating will free us both, John. You'll be able to be the person you are and it'll be the same for me. We've had so many memorable adventures together, but in recent years we've grown apart and we both know it.'

And he could not disagree. I never doubted that the decision would be best for both of us, but there was a sense of loss and sadness from which there was no escape. Part of me felt responsible for what I had done, but I reminded myself that we were both accountable for this. And by having the courage to reclaim my freedom, I had also offered John his.

My mother had little idea of the rift that had developed between us, so I wanted to tell her in person. I realised how concerned she would be about a second marriage breaking up, so I wanted to reassure her. When I arrived in Cambridge, she flung open her arms and hugged me tight before motioning me to sit down for lunch. The table was already laid with a glass of wine waiting and I realised how much she valued my visits now that my father had died. After having some of her carrot and orange soup, I broached the subject of my relationship with John. She listened attentively and then surprised me. She said that when she and my father came to our wedding, they had met a retired couple who expressed their doubt that the marriage would last more than two or three years.

'They commented on how different you and John were. We were inclined to agree, but you proved us wrong. In many respects, it's been a very successful marriage as you've achieved so much together... and you've waited to separate until the children had left home.'

It was true. Having spent a year travelling around Australia, Abi had met someone and was planning on marrying and staying there. Charlotte was now at university and spending a year at the Scripps Institute in San Diego, and Rachel had now settled in Spain.

But despite reassuring my mother that I was content to live on my own, she was concerned about me spending the rest of my days alone. So I told her about David and, although I did not know where our relationship was heading, at least I had someone whose company I enjoyed and with whom I shared interests. My mother was relieved. She had seen David as a patient when she came to stay and liked him enormously. Surprised at how easily the conversation flowed as we talked about relationships beginning and ending, I found the courage to broach a subject that was preying on my mind.

'Mum, is Teresa Bob's daughter?' I asked.

Her breath quickened. She appeared shaken and confused. I wondered if the shock had been too much for her, but I could not take back my question now. Initially she did not speak but kept taking in little gasps of air. I remained still and waited, giving her time to adjust to the realisation that her youngest daughter knew that this was a possibility. After a while her breathing calmed and she stuttered the words, 'Yes... she could be.'

I waited a few moments to see if she would say more, but she went quiet again. After a while she spoke, but took the conversation in a different direction.

'Sebastian is the one who is most like the David family. He has their characteristics – intelligent, but introverted and self-absorbed. I remember Dick taking him on a botanising trip to Scotland and he commented that Sebastian spent most of the time reading in the tent. Never again, said Dick when he returned. But of course we know of Sebastian's love of botany now.'

I wondered why she had not expanded on her initial answer and I sensed she was holding back. But I did not know what else to ask so the conversation came to an end. However, I reassured myself that at least someone in our family had raised the subject before she died.

As John and I went our separate ways, the connection between David and me grew stronger. I would stay with him for a night during the week and at the weekend he would visit me in Dent. Times together were spent walking the fells, making meals together, ice-skating when the tarns froze and talking late into the night. We had so much of our lives to catch up on. And as time went by, David became increasingly involved with the Centre so, when the United Reformed Church asked if we would take over the chapel too, I had him to support me. Initially I was hesitant about taking on the responsibility of such a large building but, with a generous grant from English Heritage, David and I began drawing up plans. He was an artist with an eye for design, so we came up with ideas as to how we could transform a dark, dank chapel into an uplifting, inspirational place. With the help of a talented young architect, the finished result won an award and it did not take long before it was heralded as being a centre of excellence for teaching meditation.

As my mother witnessed the Meditation Centre's success, she began telling friends and colleagues of her youngest daughter's achievements. I recognised there had been a profound shift in our relationship. She no longer tried to exert her influence over decisions I took, but respected me for who I was and what I was offering the community. As a result we grew closer and talked freely about subjects that she might otherwise have avoided. She liked the fact that I did not judge people for their actions but was more curious to know the reasons for them. Nevertheless, I was aware that there was still a part of me that feared her. Every Sunday morning she phoned around ten o'clock and, as I sat with a cup of coffee waiting for her call, I could feel apprehension growing.

'It's like Pavlov's dogs,' David smiled. 'You know your mother's going to phone so you get stomach ache and run off to the loo. It's a conditioned reaction.'

It was true. Waiting for her call always made me nervous, even though the conversations were only about what we had been doing during the week. I also realised that when she and I were together, I was always careful about what I said or did, in case it triggered an emotional outburst.

David was confused. 'I don't understand. You have no problem giving radio and television interviews, running courses and retreats, giving talks to hundreds of people, yet you're still nervous of your mother. It shows how deep these patterns run and control us throughout our lives.'

And I could recognise that he was right, but was at a loss to know what to do.

But as my mother got older, I felt increasingly protective of her and made sure I visited her regularly. David always came too and while there, he checked the alignment of her back as periodically it gave her trouble. She was now approaching ninety and, although she was fit and well, age was beginning to tell. Her closest friends had now passed on and increasingly she relied upon Marni for company and support. At weekends, they would go to the cinema together, discuss the latest political wrangles over a drink and talk about whatever books they were reading.

'Was Marni always your closest friend?' I asked curiously.

'No, it would be Tess. Since university days, we've always been close. I could talk to her about anything.'

When staying, I encouraged her to invite Marni for supper so I could help cook and David could accompany her home. On one occasion he did not return until long after my mother was in bed. I asked what had taken him so long.

'Marni kept stopping – not because she needed to but because she was telling a story and wanted to finish it before we arrived at her house. It was about Nora and Bob's relationship.'

'Tell me more,' I said and over a cup of tea he related the story.

'Clearly she wanted to get something off her chest and felt able to talk to me, maybe because I was not directly involved. She began by saying how much she values Nora as a friend, but the way she treated Dick during their marriage has always troubled Marni. She talked about how brazen Nora was in the way she carried on her affair with Bob, without any consideration for Dick's feelings. Friends hated seeing the way she treated him and agreed that something had to be said but, whenever the opportunity arose, no one had the courage to confront her. On one occasion, Bob invited Nora to go with him to Antibes and she insisted on going even though it was clearly inappropriate. At the time Marni's mother was staying, and when she heard about Nora's behaviour, she was so appalled that she determined to confront her, but the next time she saw her, she too reneged. It seems that everyone was intimidated by your mother, not just you.'

David paused to take my hand before continuing. 'Eventually Marni realised that the only person who could stop her was Dick, so she asked him why he allowed her to behave in the way she did.'

'And what did he say?' I asked, intrigued.

'He simply said: Nora is my Albertine. So Marni went on to explain that she's a character in a Proust novel who abandons convention and disregards the sexual mores of the day to live the life she wants. So it seems Dick adored Nora for who she was and did not wish to change her.'

I remained silent. Part of me wondered whether this was my father's excuse for not having the courage to confront her, or maybe he genuinely wanted her to have the freedom to express her sexuality and *joie de vivre*. But now he was not here to ask.

A Meeting of Hearts

It was unusual for my siblings and I to come together as my brothers were rarely in England, but we all wanted to be there for my mother's ninetieth birthday. Once again, Cornwall was chosen as the venue. Since retiring, Tony and Teresa had made the Cornish house their permanent residence and we wanted to see the changes they had made. But as my mother now found it difficult to cope with large numbers of people, she only wanted her children and Marni there, promising to give her eleven grandchildren and their spouses lunch at the House of Lords at a later date. They all adored her, but I noticed how differently she treated them to her own children, always showing genuine concern and kindness and helping them in any way she could.

A celebratory dinner was arranged for the evening and during the day my mother wanted to walk along the cliffs from Polzeath to Lundy Bay. The weather was fine and along the way, we had views of Port Isaac, Tintagel and Devon beyond. As we walked, we fell into different groups, with Nic staying close to my mother. She was now less steady on her feet, but it was a testament to her vitality and determination that she made it to her favourite picnic spot without much effort. From there she watched the waves breaking on the beach and talked about her surfing days, which only recently had ceased, as she had difficulty getting up after catching a wave. In the evening, we toasted her health with Camel Valley champagne and we cooked her favourite meal – poached salmon with homemade mayonnaise. I had rarely seen my mother so joyous and radiant, laughing at the slightest joke, delighted to have all her children around her.

But I had heard that when someone reaches the age of ninety, the ageing process accelerates. My mother confessed that on more than one occasion she had lost her balance and fallen when going to the bathroom at night. This became more serious when she was unable to get up and spent hours shivering on the bedroom floor. It was not until morning that she managed to crawl to her bedside table and phone for help. When we heard the news, David and I drove south and found her resting at Marni's house. After talking to the doctor, we decided to take her to hospital and asked if she could be admitted for tests. But a few days later she was discharged, with no cause for the fall being found. The only change to her routine was our insistence that she wear an alarm around her neck in case she fell again.

The incident, however, prompted Wanda to confide that my mother occasionally returned from the House of Lords having had a tumble. This seemed to happen when either my mother was tired or she had been to the bar for a drink. However, one evening Wanda became alarmed when she appeared with blood-stained clothes and cuts on her legs, which she had to clean up and bandage. After this, the family agreed it was unfair to expect Wanda to take on this responsibility, so we persuaded my mother to rent a room close to the Houses of Parliament, where peers stayed during the week.

Nevertheless it was still a shock when I heard that my mother had fallen the full length of an escalator in the House of Lords and had been taken to St Thomas's Hospital. We were told that there was damage to her back and severe lacerations on her shins, but our immediate concern was how she would manage when she returned to Cambridge. I organised some carers while Teresa began looking for nursing homes in Cornwall. My mother had always maintained that she never wanted to be a burden on her family and was willing to go into a home if the need arose.

In the meantime she came to stay with David and me to convalesce, keen to see the old farmhouse that we had recently bought and renovated. But as a sign of her independence, she insisted on coming by train. When she arrived, I could see her relief in knowing that she was going to be taken care of and all her needs would be met. The mornings included a visit to the doctor to have her dressings changed, walks around the garden when we showed her how to use two walking poles, and in the afternoon she would settle herself in the sitting room to read the paper or watch television. In the evening, she had her customary drink before supper, and then relaxed over a meal, which was always accompanied by a glass of wine.

I had no qualms about asking her what had caused the fall, whether she had tripped or been walking down the escalator when it was moving.

'Truly, I wasn't,' she promised. 'I can remember getting on the escalator and the next thing I knew I was spreadeagled at the bottom.'

'Do you think it could have been a slight stroke?' I suggested.

'Yes, I think it's a possibility,' she admitted honestly.

So I presumed it was not the first, and this could have been the reason for her other falls too. But despite the ease and openness of our conversations, I still found myself treading carefully, aware of a possible outburst of anger or agitation. David was right. There was still a deep-seated fear within me of being on the receiving end of her temper. But sometimes events were beyond my control. Late one afternoon, David had given a treatment to a woman from the village and, as he was seeing her out, she paused on the doorstep to ask him something. My mother, irritated by the length of the conversation, said within earshot, 'Get rid of her, Elizabeth.'

I was thrown as I knew Margaret must have overheard. My mother then went on to complain about the delay in getting supper, venting her impatience on me in any way she could. In an attempt to reassure her, I quickly ushered her into the kitchen and closed the door – but the incident disturbed me. Later that evening, when clearing the table, she snapped at me again for the way I was using a dish cloth. I reminded myself that she was vulnerable, fearful of what the future held, and it was understandable that she would take it out on me. But once again I was aware of the repercussions of her anger, not just on me but others too. When Margaret returned for a follow-up treatment, she talked to David about what had happened.

'How can anyone speak to Eliza like that? She wouldn't harm a fly. No one should treat their daughter in that way.'

And there were tears in her eyes as she spoke.

It was not long after my mother's visit north that David and I went to see how she was managing in Cambridge. The first thing we noticed was that she was struggling to get up out of a chair. She confessed that she was getting pain in her hip, so David used her bed as a treatment table to examine her. When he appeared, he was alarmed.

'We'll have to get her X-rayed straightaway.'

'What did you find?'

'It's more what I felt… bone grating against bone. I know what an arthritic hip feels like, but this is infinitely worse. I haven't come across anything like it in forty years of practice.'

I arranged for my mother to see a specialist and X-rays revealed that the ball of the femur had punched a hole through the socket of her hip joint. We presumed it had happened at the time of accident and the doctors had not picked it up. For speed, she was operated on privately and she convalesced in a Cambridge nursing home. But again I realised my mother's strength of character. For months she had endured severe pain and had never complained, sought sympathy or played the victim, and had been determined to carry on regardless.

However, it was soon clear that my mother would never make a full recovery, so she agreed to move to a nursing home close to the Cornish house. We arranged for a few favourite pieces of furniture to go with her, she said her farewells to her colleagues at the House of Lords and made the journey from Cambridge to Cornwall for the last time. But as the Cambridge house had to be cleared and sold, and we wanted to ensure my mother was settling into her new home, journeys to the south became more frequent.

Only when all had been successfully accomplished, was I able to return my attention to the Meditation Centre. But before long, my mother began putting pressure on me to go to Cornwall to pay her another visit, despite Teresa seeing her regularly. After several phone calls when my mother stated in no uncertain terms that I was putting the Centre before her, I felt compelled to put pen to paper. In a measured but firm way, I reminded her of the numerous trips I had made south and that I also had the Centre to run and courses to host. It took courage to write, but a shift had taken place within me and I knew it was time to say, 'No.' Her behaviour was serving neither her nor anyone else. I received a reply by return post, written in shaky handwriting:

> *My darling,*
> *I'm so very sorry. I've behaved like a pig. I can't bear the way I have treated you. Forgive me. Come when you can and there's no pressure. I love you my darling, Mum*

I was astonished. I had never in my life heard her apologise before, nor say that she loved me. I also realised that in referring to herself as a pig, she would be carrying feelings of guilt. In one letter, the hurt and resentment that had been present throughout my life melted away in a moment. After receiving it, I arranged a time to go and visit her and she appreciated every moment. With help, she was still able to walk the short distance to the cliff top to watch the waves and together we sorted through her clothes and wrote some letters. Such times were tender, relaxed, and she seemed settled and content at last. It appeared that she had made friends in the nursing home and also had the occasional visit from a fellow peer.

A couple of years passed without any mishap and then for my birthday, she suggested taking David, Tony, Teresa and me for lunch at Rick Stein's fish restaurant in Padstow. It was a favourite haunt of my family as my parents had found it long before it achieved television fame. After lunch, we took her back to the nursing home and I could tell that she was relieved to be back. She was now having intermittent pains in her stomach and a small tumour had been found in her bowel but, at the age of ninety-seven, it was thought best not to intervene.

It was only a couple of weeks later that a nurse phoned to say they had found my mother unconscious and she had been taken in an ambulance to the hospital in Truro. As Tony and Teresa were on holiday in Italy, I kept in touch, but it was difficult to get any clear diagnosis. Septicaemia was suspected but the doctor said they would be operating that afternoon. By early evening I managed to talk to the anaesthetist, who assured me that my mother was comfortable, but from the tone of his voice I was doubtful. So I approached my nephew Ivo, a consultant at Nottingham Hospital, who managed to get hold of the surgeon.

'I don't think the prognosis is good,' he told me. 'I'm going to drive down tonight. We had plans to go anyway as I wanted to tell her that we're expecting our first child.'

I congratulated him on the news and said I would go too. It was nine o'clock at night and I was prepared to set off alone as the previous weekend David had been in hospital after a mountain bike accident. With thirty stitches in his forehead and a spinal fracture, I assumed he would not want to travel but, taking me in his arms, he insisted, 'It's an eight-hour drive and raining hard. I'm coming.'

It was five in the morning when we arrived at the dimly lit hospital in Truro. There was no one at reception, no doctor nor nurse in sight and the building felt eerie. Ivo had told me my mother had been kept in the recovery room after the operation as she was not well enough to move. As we made our way through a maze of corridors, we looked for signs to the operating theatre and eventually came across a nurse who took us through some swing doors – and there was my mother, draped in tubes and wires attached to different monitors with Ivo and his wife sitting beside her. As soon as my mother saw us she found the energy to fling open her arms and welcomed us with a hug and broad smile. But as she did not have her hearing aids it was difficult to talk, so I settled myself on the edge of the bed, aware that she was having difficulty breathing.

'Can't you do something?' I asked the nurse. 'Why is she gasping like that?'

'My dear, your mother's very poorly, but I can give her a sedative. That should help her.'

Soon my mother began to breathe more easily and I took her hand, looked into her eyes and she looked into mine. We must have stayed like this for half an hour or more, communing with each other in silence. I wanted to tell her how much I loved her, how grateful I was for all the times we had spent together, even though she had challenged me more than anyone else in my life. I knew it was just a matter of time before she would go and it was a relief to have Ivo there to guide and support us. As a consultant, he was able to suggest that my mother was detached from a couple of monitors and this simple gesture gave her back her dignity.

I watched as my mother's attention was drawn to some screens at the end of her bed that were decorated with paintings of seascapes, cliffs, rock pools and brightly coloured fish. She allowed her gaze to wander from one scene to the next like an enchanted child, becoming mesmerised by the different shapes, colours and patterns. It was as though she was savouring every last moment of the delights of this world before leaving it. When her focus shifted away from the murals, she looked back at me, and from the expression on her face, I could see that she had found peace at last. All the restlessness and agitation had gone. There was just an indefinable presence, a sense of stillness, which encompassed us both in a loving embrace. I knew what a privilege it was to stand by her side at the portal between life and death, two people whose lives had been inextricably linked but were soon to be parted.

My reverie was interrupted by a nurse bringing us some tea and toast.

'How long?' I whispered to Ivo.

'You can never tell. At some point she'll have to be moved as they'll begin the day's operations. I'm not sure how she'll take that.'

But instead of the change of scene upsetting her, my mother perked up as she was wheeled through corridors, in and out of lifts, and taken into a private room. As we re-settled ourselves in our new surroundings, David and I held her hands as we sat either side of the bed. After a while my mother closed her eyes, so I closed mine and saw an image of my father as a young man, dressed in a suit waiting for her with arms outstretched. A knock at the door brought me back. It was the surgeon who had come to tell us about the operation and explain what they had found. But while engaged in conversation, his registrar interrupted, 'I think she's going. We'll leave you now.'

I turned to my mother and heard her breath becoming fainter, more intermittent, and then one last lingering sigh and she was gone. There were no tears, just a profound sense of gratitude that I had been with her at the end. We waited until the life force ebbed away and then I put my hand on her heart and kissed her on her forehead.

It was late morning when we left the hospital and our immediate thought was food. As we sat in a pub overlooking Padstow harbour having fish pie and a glass of cider, we watched the sun emerge from behind some rain clouds and cast a pool of silvery white light on the sea.

Teresa and Tony returned the following day in disbelief that they had been away when my mother had been taken ill.

Teresa recalled, 'I called in to see her before we went and she was smiling and buoyant, so that's how I'll remember her.'

We stayed for a couple of days to help with the funeral arrangements but, as was the case with my father, we had to wait for my brothers to fly over from Canada. As my mother wanted a memorial service held at Newnham College, we decided to invite only family and close friends to the crematorium. We chose a sea grass coffin and, as with my father, I took the responsibility of garlanding it with flowers. Her grandsons carried it into the crematorium and as soon as I saw it, I let out a cry. It looked so beautiful, a fitting accolade for my mother. They were the first tears I had shed since her passing so to settle myself, I turned my gaze to the large window behind the altar. It was an uplifting scene – the sky was blue and the wooded valley was bathed in winter sunlight. My two brothers spoke, Teresa read a poem and I gave the tribute to my mother. I talked about her social skills, her love of entertaining, energy and enthusiasm for whatever life had to offer and her gift of bringing people together. I then went on to say that it was not easy being her daughter.

'She was a strict disciplinarian with high standards, so my personal experience of her was like being tempered in a fire. But without her influence, I wouldn't be the person I am today. With passion she embraced the outer world, while I was drawn to an inner one, but in poignant synchronicity the two came together in the end.'

Then I turned towards the coffin, put my hands together and whispered, '*Namaste.*'

Before returning to my seat, I glanced out of the window and saw a buzzard circling high in the sky, a perfect symbol of freedom.

After the funeral, one of the carers from the nursing home came and put her arms around me.

'I just want to tell you how much your mother loved you and

how proud she was of all you've done. I know because of the way she spoke about you, so never forget that, my dear.'

And in that brief, unexpected exchange, I felt at peace. There was no sense of loss or longing, just immense gratitude that there had been completion with my mother at last.

BACK TO MY SEARCH

~

I realised it was time for me to move on from the Meditation Centre. The responsibility of running the Centre was taking its toll and although I loved inspiring others on their spiritual journey, I was now in need of guidance myself. In my years of searching, I had never been drawn to any religion or belief system but wanted to discover the universal truths that underpinned them all. However, I had always looked to the East as my meditation and spiritual practices came from those traditions. I knew little of the Western esoteric traditions that not only included the wisdom of Sufism and the Kabbalah, but also the mystical teachings of Christ Yeshua.

A Franciscan brother shared his thoughts: 'The essence of Christ's teaching is the mystery of love, the truth that lies at the heart of all religions. That's where your search begins.'

I began to reflect. What happened all that time ago? Why had the essence of Christ's teaching become lost in a plethora of dogma, creeds and beliefs? I was drawn to go back in time, explore the gnostic gospels and discover the timeless truths that Christ came to impart to free humanity from fear and suffering. With David I travelled to Palestine to see the landscape where Yeshua lived and taught. We stayed in the Old City of Jerusalem, before moving north to the Sea of Galilee and Safed, the home of the ancient

Hebraic mystical teachings. I acquainted myself with Aramaic, the language that Yeshua spoke, and discovered translations of ancient texts that talked about the need to transcend the ego in order to experience the infinite power of love.

After months of research and time spent deepening my own experience of the inner mysteries, I felt inspired to write again. I wanted to tell a story of two women living two millennia apart – one from the English Lake District and the other from Bethany in Palestine. They are both called Martha, tread similar paths, and are on a journey to find the truth of themselves and the truth of love. I called the book *The Mystery of Martha*, and to mark its publication, I wanted to bring the whole family together. My mother had always been the hub around whom the children, grandchildren and great-grandchildren always gravitated. Now she was gone, there was a danger of us losing touch with one another. I was also aware that within my immediate family, I rarely saw my daughters as we lived so far apart. Abi had been through a divorce, remarried and now had four children. Eduardo, Rachel, and their son and daughter were still living in Spain. It was only Charlotte who remained in England... living on a houseboat in Oxford.

Thirty of us came together for supper the evening before the book launch, many seeing each other for the first time in years. There was joy and excitement as we gathered, relieved that it was for a celebration rather than a funeral. But for me the greatest pleasure was seeing my children again. Each one of them nourished me in their own unique way and I was reminded how much I missed their presence in my life.

While the family was staying, Teresa and I talked about our nanny Joan, who in recent years had visited our respective homes. She was keen to connect again with the two girls she had once looked after. Recalling those times with fondness, she told us that she wished she had not left us when she did. Her marriage had failed and she now regarded her years in Cambridge as some of the happiest of her life. She loved to reminisce, telling stories about the past and the famous people she met while living with my parents. But she was now quite frail, so my sister and I decided to go to her home in Kent and take her out for lunch.

Teresa was ebullient, glad that we had made the arrangement and offered to pay for us all. In customary style she ordered a bottle of Sauvignon Blanc and, over a three-course lunch, Joan regaled us with stories about the plays we did at Hampton Court, my love of the maze and summers we spent in Cornwall. I then asked Joan how she had coped with my mother's temper.

'It never bothered me as behind that sharp tongue, I knew there was someone who cared. But I felt sorry for you, Eliza. You always got the short straw. If Teresa was naughty and you copied her, it was always you who got the blame.'

I looked at my sister. 'You were more confident and outgoing than me. I think Mum liked you better.'

Joan consoled me. 'By the time you came along, Eliza, I think she was more interested in her own career than taking care of her children.'

Then Joan went on to talk about people she remembered and among them was Bob. 'How you all loved it when he came to stay. He brought smiles to your faces... especially your mother,' Joan chuckled.

'So were they lovers?' my sister asked.

'There was certainly something between them. I know 'cos I heard them kissing on the landing.'

Such conversations made me think about the past and wonder how long my mother's affair with Bob had lasted. Joan had often said how alike Teresa and Bob were, both physically and emotionally, whereas I was more like my father – quieter and more inward-looking. Certainly when I asked my mother if Teresa was Bob's daughter, from her response I was convinced that she was. I also sensed Teresa thought so too, although she was reluctant to admit to it. I noticed how she always took an interest when any new book or television programme came out about Bob. At times

Teresa and I had talked about doing a DNA test, but when it came to it she seemed wary so we never pursued it.

However, an unexpected encounter reignited my curiosity about my ancestral line. Padma was a visionary and teacher whom I had met a few years earlier on a retreat in France. I valued his gifts and insights hugely. As he was visiting the Lake District, he came over to see us. It was a beautiful day so we had lunch on the terrace overlooking the dale. Unexpectedly, he looked across at me and asked, 'Eliza, why is there a block at the back of your heart?'

I was accustomed to spiritual teachers taking me unawares if they saw distortions in my energy field, but when this happened I found it unnerving.

Padma continued: 'There's a wound that needs healing and it's time it was done.'

He went on to talk about the importance of healing old scars otherwise our hearts cannot open fully.

'You're the matriarch of the family now,' he continued. 'You not only have the responsibility of healing yourself but also your ancestral line, otherwise patterns will be passed on from one generation to the next. Remember, you had father issues which are now being reflected in your children and their children too. The problems magnify in each successive generation.'

Certainly neither Rachel nor Abi had seen their father for years and I now had a great-granddaughter who did not even know who her father was. I acknowledged that Padma had a point.

He then dropped into silence for a few moments before suggesting that we went inside. As we sat around the kitchen table, he said quietly, 'I feel Christ Yeshua's presence… it's the first time I've been aware of him in a while.'

His words came as no surprise as while I had been writing *The Mystery of Martha*, I had often felt Yeshua around me. Indeed, sometimes when I was sitting with David in the evening, it seemed as though there were three of us in the room.

Then speaking quietly, Padma said, 'Yeshua's showing me three black pebbles in the palm of his hand. It seems there's been a betrayal in your family, Eliza. What could it be?'

I had no idea what Padma was talking about so shook my head.

'Close your eyes. Let your mind journey inwards. What do you see?'

At first there was darkness, but after a little while I realised that I was in a tunnel that felt strange and sinister. No one was there.

'Look more closely,' Padma guided me. 'What's happening?'

I peered into the abyss and some shadowy figures appeared. They seemed to be involved in something secretive. I felt uncomfortable and told him so.

'What are they doing?' Padma persisted.

Gradually the scene took on more clarity.

'Something sexual,' I said, 'but they are disguising it.'

'And what part are you playing?'

'None, as far as I can tell.'

'But are you there?'

'Yes… observing, but I'm not a part of it.'

'Bearing witness to a deception and keeping quiet makes you complicit too. There's been a sexual betrayal in your ancestral line and Yeshua is showing me that you are the one who can heal it.'

I was bewildered. For years I had been struggling to heal the wounds within myself, never mind those that were carried by others in the past. In the following days, I kept remembering what Padma had said and wondering how I could find out more. Each time I took my mind to the betrayal, I sensed the presence of my grandmother around me, my father's mother. I remembered her as a woman of honour and integrity and believed she might hold the key to information that I needed. I looked through some old photographs and found one taken on the Cornish cliffs of my grandmother, her mother, husband, my father and, at the centre of the group was my mother with her hair clipped back and wearing dark glasses. She looked beautiful, like a film star, but her expression was pensive, as though she was in a world of her own. Then I noticed the date – August 1947 – and realised that at the time she was six months pregnant with me.

I needed time to assimilate what I had seen, so I went for my favourite walk up the fell, where there were views of the Dales to the east and the Lake District to the west. The dale looked magical and, as I sat on a cairn gazing into the distance, I took my mind to my grandmother and unexpectedly found myself sobbing helplessly in a way I had not done for years. It felt as though she was with me, encouraging me to uncover the mystery that lay hidden in the past. And from then on, whenever I took my attention to her, I felt an intensity of emotion that to me indicated the betrayal was linked to her ancestral line.

It was 2020 and the world was in varying degrees of lockdown, so Teresa suggested that we connect with my two brothers online to catch up with news. The last time we were together had been at my mother's funeral. After comparing notes on restrictions in Canada and Britain, we talked about how we were occupying ourselves. Reading Greek and Latin was mentioned as well as learning new choral and piano pieces and, as so often before, I felt I had little to offer to the conversation. The only contribution I made was to ask about their families and tell them about mine.

But at the beginning of one of the meetings Teresa flashed up a book titled *The Peer and the Gangster*, which had just been published. She said it told the story of Bob's life, political career and friendship with the Krays. Then she added with glee, 'And there's still no mention of Mum, nor what Bob did with the libel money from the *Sunday Mirror*.'

I was not surprised as my mother had not been mentioned in Bob's biography either. But what intrigued me was that Teresa still followed media coverage about Bob.

Shortly after this exchange, Teresa's eldest son Jason came to stay on his way to Scotland. His parents had recently sold the Cornish home and were now living in a house in Exeter, where he had stayed the previous weekend. While there, he noticed the book *The Peer and the Gangster* lying around and also wondered why Teresa had bought it. After supper, Jason gently started probing, asking me about Nora's affair with Bob and whether I thought Teresa was his daughter. I told him of my mother's response when I had asked her. I also explained how well Bob treated us as children and in many respects had been more like a father than Dick.

Jason responded, 'I saw a photo of Bob when he was young and I could not believe the similarity between him and Mum.'

'He reminds me of you too, Jason.' I smiled.

'How?'

'You're a risk taker and enjoy gambling… and you're kind, fun and sensitive. But it's not just the way you express yourself, there's also a physical resemblance between you and Bob.'

'I know I have an addictive streak. That's why I gave up alcohol and cigarettes,' Jason admitted before adding, 'It's time we found out the truth, not just for our sake but for future generations too – and we need to do it while you and Mum are alive.'

When Jason left, I was drawn to find out more about Bob – his vision, political views, his family and life in Scotland. In my research I discovered a quote from his nephew Ludovic Kennedy saying that to his certain knowledge:

> *Bob fathered at least three children by the wives of other men*
> *– two by one woman, one by another.*

I had heard about Bob's long affair with Dorothy Macmillan and that her youngest daughter Sarah was believed to be Bob's child. But her husband, Prime Minister Harold Macmillan, had taken her on as his own and the press had been respectful and kept quiet. So who were the other two children who Ludovic was referring to? He had died in 2009 so I could not ask him now. But I knew that he was a well-respected journalist with a reputation for uncovering miscarriages of justice. Surely if anyone knew the truth about Bob's affairs and offspring, it would be him. So if my hunch was right and Teresa was Bob's child, this would put my own identity in question too.

What if I were not Dick David's daughter? I had always assumed that I was, in part because I believed there were strong similarities between us, although I neither had his height nor intellect. I scribbled down my thoughts, including my latest discovery, and sent them to Jason, who agreed it was time for us to have a DNA test. However, owing to the sensitivity of the subject and Teresa's feelings, I made it clear that I wanted to talk to her first and Jason promised to honour my request. But through no fault of his, she got wind of the idea before I had a chance to see her, told my brothers about my suspicions and then the accusations began. How could I doubt my mother's impeccable reputation, the love that my parents had for one another, my sister's heritage and my own? Even my own experience of childhood was questioned and dismissed.

How well I knew that when fear takes hold, views and opinions become more entrenched and are then projected onto others. It seemed that no one could hear me, nor even was prepared to listen. I remembered Padma saying that when a betrayal occurs, remaining silent makes us culpable too and I now realised the degree of courage that was needed to expose the truth. Yet my own parentage was in doubt too – and I was left with the question: Who am I?

WHO IS MY FATHER?

~

I was confused and had no one to turn to. Maybe I was destined not to know who my father was? But it felt strange. I began reaching out, wondering who I could talk to and how a resolution could be found. Then help appeared in an unexpected form. It was Branwen, Nic's daughter, who heard of my dilemma and offered her support.

'I'm a geneticist after all,' she said. 'If you and I have a DNA test, it'll show whether we are full aunt and niece. If we're not, then you will be Nic's half-sister, which means you have different fathers.'

I appreciated Branwen's clarity and straightforward manner. She did not get enmeshed in emotion but offered a simple, practical solution. I was curious to have a DNA test anyway, as I had heard that it revealed which parts of the world our ancestors came from. At the time Rachel was staying as she and Eduardo were planning to move back to England. Branwen suggested she have a test too as the more family members who take part, the more chance there is of getting a reliable result. So Rachel and I sent off samples of saliva, knowing that it would be several weeks before the results came through.

It was a couple of days before Christmas when they arrived so we waited until Christmas Day before opening the file. With a log fire burning and lights from the tree flickering on the ceiling,

Rachel and I sat on the sofa and looked at the results. It took a while for me to find my way around the site. Rachel was quicker.

'You're 40% Scots and 12% Norwegian,' she said with surprise. 'Where did that come from, Mum?'

'I've no idea. The strange thing is that I've got no Welsh. The David family comes from Laugharne in South Wales. That's where they lived and their ancestors are buried.'

'Look, Derbyshire shows up. That's where your mum comes from, but why Yorkshire and Lancashire? I didn't know you had relations there.'

Then we moved on to look at DNA relatives. Rachel topped the list as my daughter, followed by my niece Branwen.

'You see, Branwen and I have got 11% DNA in common,' I said confidently, 'so I am a David and my father's daughter.'

'You'll have to check that,' Rachel said uncertainly.

And I disappeared into the kitchen to dish up the guinea fowl and steam some sprouts.

In truth, I did not fully understand the results, but I was so convinced that I was Dick David's daughter that I was unable to take in any information that might show otherwise. My only confusion was that I was English and Scottish with a little Irish, but there was no Welsh in me. My father's parents both had Welsh surnames, Evans and David, and I had always believed that I had Celtic roots. I told Branwen that the results had arrived and a couple of days later received an email from her clarifying the situation. I had to read it a couple of times to understand its permutations, but she explained that the DNA results showed that she and I shared only one ancestor and not two.

If you and I were full aunt-niece we would share 25% DNA and not 11%. So Nic is your half-brother and Dick is not your father. Does this make sense? I hope this doesn't come as too much of a shock for you given your initial interpretation.

I got up and walked around the kitchen a few times trying to take in the news. Then I went into the garden and gazed blankly down the dale and at the hills in the distance. I reminded myself the only reason I had wanted a DNA test was to find out where my ancestors came from and had never taken Ludovic Kennedy's comment seriously. I was in little doubt as to who my father was. How could the result possibly show otherwise? I went to tell David the news.

'Apparently Dick David is not my dad. Branwen and I don't share enough DNA for him to be my father. I've never been any good at maths.'

'So am I the only David around here now?' he said smiling. But he could see tears in my eyes and took me in his arms. 'I'm sorry... so sorry.'

'It feels strange... very strange,' I whispered. 'I no longer know who I am.'

'You're still you... the beautiful Eliza, and that'll never change.'

'But I don't know who my father is. How will I be able to track down Mum's lovers now?'

'Perhaps Ludovic Kennedy was right and you really are Bob's daughter.'

'Absolutely not,' I said emphatically. 'I'm sure Teresa's his child, but Mum would never have made the same mistake twice. You can get away with one love child, but not two.'

My first responsibility was to tell my siblings, so I called Teresa.

'That's devastating news for a Monday morning,' she said.

'For me, Teresa... not for you.'

'Maybe there's a mistake?' she asked as the information sank in.

'I don't think so.'

Sebastian had a similar reaction, querying the maths and wondering whether the result was correct. Nic took the findings more seriously as his daughter had organised the test. But at least there was agreement between us that we should all now have DNA tests to establish the truth.

As I was deliberating possibilities as to who my father might be, I remembered a newspaper article that Nic had sent the family a few weeks before. It was about my mother having been seen driving with someone called Patrick Hadley during or after the war. The article stated that as they were in a restricted area close to the Sandringham Estate, she had to pay a fine of one pound. She was reported as saying to the police, 'I didn't know the area was out of bounds. It was purely a pleasure trip.'

From the article it was apparent that she had stayed overnight with Patrick Hadley, so I asked Nic if he knew him.

'Yes, he was often at Ashton House. He was a musician, sociable and good fun. I remember Dick and Nora saw a lot of him.'

'Do you think he could have been Mum's lover?' I asked, wondering if he was my father.

'Maybe. She was clearly out enjoying herself and stayed the night with him too.'

David and I reread the article and noticed the date.

'Look,' David pointed out, 'it was 12 February when Nora stayed. That's exactly nine months before you were born. It would fit.'

Fortunately Patrick Hadley was well known in Cambridge circles and there was a book about him titled *Paddy – His Life and Times*. I discovered that he was Professor of Music at Cambridge University, a well-respected English composer and close friend of Vaughan Williams. But apparently he had lost the lower half of his leg in the First World War and drank more than he should to alleviate the pain. Nevertheless, his students adored him. He was known for his sense of humour, love of fast cars, good food and wine... all qualities that my mother enjoyed. Apparently he had never married but instead had fleeting relationships. And apart from his immediate family, the only person he remembered in his will was my mother to whom he left some vintage port and wine.

'Do you think he's my father?' I asked David.

'We need to find out the year the newspaper article was written.'

So I got in touch with the secretary of the local history society, who was intrigued by the story and keen to help. She asked to see the back of the newspaper article, thinking it might offer some clues as to the year of its publication… and then we waited.

Meanwhile, I began imagining Patrick Hadley as my mother's lover and my father. From what I had read, he had a melancholic streak that was expressed through his musical compositions. He was dark-haired and small like me, a lover of the hills, seascapes and nature, and regarded himself to be a seeker. Yes, these were all characteristics with which I could identify. It was a couple of weeks before we heard back from the secretary of the History Society, who said that it was the advertisement on the back of the article that gave the date away.

'It was for a shop that closed down in 1942, so we were able to trace the article to February 1941. That was when your mother stayed with Patrick Hadley.'

It was six years before I was born. If my mother had an affair with him, it would have been early on in the war. Once again, I was thrown into a state of confusion.

My next move was to begin contacting DNA relatives who appeared as cousins on the Heritage site. John Somerville was listed as my third cousin. I liked the name so sent him a message, explaining that I had no idea who my father and was wondering how we were related. Within a few days he replied with a list of surnames found in his ancestral line – Fermoy, Roche, Boothby, Goschen, Dent and Somerville. It made no sense. Why was the name Boothby there? Of course, I reasoned, Boothby was probably a common name. There must be plenty of Boothbys in the world apart from the one I knew. No doubt it was a coincidence. That evening I told Rachel about John Somerville's message.

'I was just getting use to Patrick Hadley being my grandfather,' she laughed, 'and now it seems it could be Bob. At least I knew him and he had a big heart. Let's drink to Bob,' she said, raising her glass.

I took my mind back to Ludovic Kennedy's comment but persisted in questioning its truth. Why were Teresa and I so different? We were unalike physically, mentally and emotionally, and she had no spiritual leanings whatsoever. Her philosophy of life was like Bob: *Eat, drink and be merry, for tomorrow we may die.*

I recalled being with her in Greece the previous year when she had asked the hotel owner if she and I were similar.

'No,' the woman replied at once. 'I would never have guessed you were sisters.'

As for Bob and me, we had even less in common. I loved his company but simply could not believe that he was my father. All I could do was continue with my investigations and contact more DNA relatives, explaining my predicament. It was not long before I had more replies – all of which were sympathetic and helpful. Clovis and Justin Meath-Baker said they were descendants of the Patterson family and were related to Bob on his mother's side. Amanda Trotter was a cousin of Bob on his paternal side and from her photograph, looked very like Teresa. Every lead I followed up took me back to Bob's parents, grandparents, great-grandparents and beyond. The evidence was mounting, but I still found it hard to assimilate the news.

I thought of the time that Teresa was conceived early in 1944. It was during the war when my father was away in the Navy and Bob had temporarily been drafted to Cambridge. The circumstances would fit. I then wondered about my own conception three years later. Dick had then returned from the war having had a severe bout of hepatitis. He had served on a ship that had been torpedoed and sunk and also lost his brother, which must have affected him emotionally. Presumably he had also found out that my mother was having an affair and that Teresa was her lover's child. It is well known that those on active service suffer from post-traumatic stress, so maybe it took time for Dick to recover from the trauma of the war, and my mother continued her affair with Bob?

But accepting the reality that I was Bob's daughter was a challenge. Emotions surfaced that I found hard to reconcile. I kept seeing myself as the unwanted child, the runt of the litter, the daughter whom my mother had resented because I should have been Dick's child – his prize after all he had gone through during the war. I was a mistake. I was the wrong child, which was exactly how I had felt all my life. The only difference was that now I knew why. No wonder my mother had taken her anger out on me. Every time she looked at me, I would have mirrored back her guilt. I neither had Dick's knowledge and intellectual capacity, nor showed much interest in his hobbies and passions. I reached out to Sebastian and told him how I felt. He listened attentively before saying in a reassuring manner, 'Don't jump to conclusions, Eliza. Wait until we get more results. Nothing is certain yet.'

He was right. But from the tone in his voice, I knew that he too was having difficulty in reconciling himself with this strange turn of events.

As the weeks went by, I became impatient for answers so I contacted a genealogist. She suggested having a test with a different site to find more second, third and fourth cousins. She explained the importance of building up a comprehensive family tree as this is the most accurate way to determine our ancestors. Meanwhile, the uncertainty was testing the family in different ways and tension grew as we waited for more news.

Sebastian's results came in first and once again shock reverberated through the family. It confirmed that he and I shared only one parent, making him my half-brother – and as Branwen reminded us, her test already showed that Nic was my half-brother too.

When Teresa's results finally came through, it not only showed that we were full sisters but that we shared 58% DNA, an unusually high proportion for siblings. So now we had to face the reality that our family comprised Dick, who had two sons with my mother, and my mother who had two sons with him and two daughters with someone else... whom we now presumed to be Bob. But our suspicions had to be confirmed professionally. So the genealogist offered to complete the family tree and analyse the results. Another wait, and then finally during a one-hour consultation she explained in depth that her analysis revealed that there was no shadow of doubt that Teresa and I were Bob Boothby's daughters.

'So why are we so unalike?' I asked.

'Many factors are involved,' she explained. 'Look at the vastness of your heritage and all the influences that have been passed down. There are also behavioural and environmental factors to take into account too. From the moment we are born we have very different experiences even though we are brought up within the same family. None of us know what makes us who we are. It's a mystery and is probably best kept that way.'

I felt compassion for my sister. She now had no choice but to accept the truth of her parentage. A suspicion that had haunted her since teenage years had at last become a reality. I could understand why she wanted to be Dick's daughter as I felt the same, but it was no longer an option to go on pretending that we were Davids when we were not. We now had to readjust to the news and let go of long-held beliefs, not just for our own sakes but for our children and their children too.

My brothers' sadness was the timing of my mother's betrayal. They discovered some letters from Dick to my mother during the war revealing that he was back in Portsmouth at the time Teresa was conceived. And my mother visited him while he was there... probably pregnant at the time. And I was conceived shortly after Dick had been demobbed so he had not been home for long. Consequently, it was the circumstances of my mother's infidelities that they found most difficult to reconcile.

When my results came through from the second heritage site, I discovered more relatives – the Kennedys and Careys, who I remembered from days at Hampton Court and were all my cousins. As Bob came from a distinguished family, I was fortunate that his ancestral line was well documented on both the maternal and paternal sides, with family members having made their mark in business, banking, the arts, politics and journalism. I was also able to trace relations as far back as the sixteenth century.

As I continued with my research, I felt sympathy for those who have no idea who their father is, nor any way of finding out. To be left in a state of not knowing would surely cast a shadow over one's life that would be difficult to erase.

But exposing the truth had repercussions within the family. Conflicting feelings surfaced and my siblings suggested we cease communication for a while to allow us time to assimilate the news. But before this happened, my sister said that she had found a letter from Bob that mentioned me. I asked to see it, but she never sent it. Then weeks later I received a copy of just one of its pages with no message attached:

> Teresa, I just want you to know that I have cared for you more than anyone else in my life and my feelings about you are quite unchanged. I wish I could say the same for Elizabeth...

Bob went on to say how welcome she would be at Eaton Square and that he would love to visit her in Birmingham and meet her children too. After reading it, I sat quietly. I wanted to absorb its content without emotion interfering. I had always known that Bob loved Teresa more than me, but I had reasoned this was natural as she was his goddaughter... or possible daughter. But the goal posts had now changed and I was his daughter too. As I watched my feelings ebb and flow, I was relieved that the familiar sense of rejection no longer had such a hold on me. Instead, I felt compassion for both Bob and my sister. He had loved her deeply, maybe more than any other woman in his life, yet he had never been able to express the truth of his feelings, nor talk about their father-daughter relationship. And as I well knew, when feelings are repressed, misunderstandings can occur.

As for me, I now wanted to get to know my father – not as a political figure, radio and television star, or someone who liked partying and befriending questionable characters – but the man behind the public persona. Who was the real Bob Boothby? What traits and qualities had I inherited from him? I also wanted to bring back honour to the family name. After all, I was a Boothby too.

A Need to Be Loved

⤳

I would never have imagined that I was conceived at Eaton Square. The month would have been February so, as Bob's birthday was on the twelfth, my mother may have been there for a celebration and I was the result. I had little doubt that she knew whose child she was carrying as a woman generally intuits who the true father is. I had some letters from Bob in the attic and wondered if they held any clues. As I began sorting through boxes, I came across one that my brother had given me after clearing my mother's house. In it there was an envelope labelled *Elizabeth's Birth*. It contained congratulatory telegrams, cards and letters from friends and family, and among them there were three from Bob. Firstly a telegram saying:

Splendid, splendid, splendid.

Then a postcard:

I am so pleased. I hope it didn't hurt too much. You must take it very easy for a fortnight and I look forward to seeing you on the 22nd. Blessings to you both, Bob

Lastly there was a letter mentioning how delighted he was that I was going to be called 'Elizabeth Sarah' as they were his favourite names. He then went on to say how much he was looking forward to seeing me in three days' time. From the tone of the correspondence, it certainly suggested that Bob was celebrating the birth of his second daughter.

I then found a more formal letter from Dick, agreeing with the names and my mother's choice of godparents. As I rummaged through more papers, I found letters from Bob that he sent to me in my teenage years, addressing me as *'precious pussy-cat'* and *'clever little girl'*. There were also cards joking about how much money he had lost in Monte Carlo, that he had bathed in a heated pool and was betting that my mother would soon be Mayor of Cambridge, adding, *'and then she'll have no time for me'*.

But who was the man behind the public persona? That was what I wanted to find out. I started my research by buying the books he wrote – *I Fight to Live* published in 1947, the year of my birth; *My Yesterday, Your Tomorrow* and *Recollections of a Rebel*, which was written eight years before he died. I also bought his biography, *A Portrait of Bob Boothby* and *The Peer and the Gangster*, the book that sparked Jason's curiosity to find out the truth. Then I steeled myself to watch two documentaries, *The Gangster and the Pervert Peer* and *Lords of the Underworld*.

I wondered how I would feel knowing more about this side of Bob's character. When growing up, I knew him as someone who gave gifts and brought joy to our family, as a respected politician and popular television and radio personality. But it was now clear that later in life, he attended debauched parties in Soho with celebrities and high-ranking politicians, and also befriended East End gangsters. In the early sixties, I also discovered that Bob also had a brief relationship with a young man called Leslie Holt that his family described as warm and affectionate – and it was he who introduced Bob to the Kray twins.

Bob's friendship with the Krays seems to have been based around their mutual liking for young, good-looking, adult men. Contrary to what was later suggested, Bob was not drawn sexually to those who were underage. He was loving and kind and would never have wanted to harm or abuse anyone. Nor did he have a sexual relationship with either of the Krays. It was simply that occasionally after a night out, they would procure a young man for Bob to take home. And when the *Sunday Mirror* story broke, Bob's friendship with the Krays ended promptly, along with his brief return to homosexuality. He then turned his attention to Wanda Sanna, whom he had met several years before, had always wanted to marry, and finally she agreed to become his wife. In total, his friendship with the Kray brothers lasted barely two years, so what about the other eighty-four years of his life?

In his biography there were photos of him and his family at different stages in his life. I had never seen any physical resemblance between Bob and me, but in a picture of his mother Mabel I recognised my mouth, eyes and the shape of my face. I also saw a likeness between her and my daughter Charlotte, and she was struck by the similarity too. Mabel was described as a woman of wit and grace, a good listener, someone who enjoyed entertaining, but was also determined and strong-minded. I could certainly identify with some of those characteristics, although she had a penchant for gambling and I did not.

I then discovered that we did once meet. My mother had been diligent in recording the milestones of her children's lives and, despite reading my baby book many times, there was one entry I had never understood. For some reason when I was nine months old, my mother had taken me to Beechwood in Edinburgh and I had never known why. From reading Bob's biography, however, I had now learned that it was his family home – a grand eighteenth-century house with twenty acres of land on Corstorphine Hill, which his parents had bought in 1906.

From what my mother had written, it seems that her au pair had left and, while waiting for another, Bob suggested us going to Beechwood for a month. We stayed the night at Bob's flat before travelling by train to Edinburgh where Mabel, who was then eighty years old, was delighted to see us. While there, Florence the cook and Mabel's two maids, Meta and Mary, helped look after me and my mother wrote:

Elizabeth came on in leaps and bounds and looked splendidly healthy when we returned south.

That was the only time I met my grandmother as she passed away the following year. Her husband Robert, known as Tom, had died six years previously. It was apparent that Bob adored him, saying that he was the handsomest man in Edinburgh, that he loved writing poetry, entertaining guests with stories and song, and was an excellent sportsman too. Bob always maintained he could never equal his father, describing him as a close friend and confidante, whom he loved and admired deeply. In later years, Bob also mused that he and his parents may have loved one another too much, which might have given him unrealistic expectations when it came to romantic relationships.

But reading about Bob told only part of the story. I wanted to meet his relations, as they were now my family too. Simon Carey and Ludovic Kennedy, both second cousins, had died within the last fifteen years, but Simon had three children: Carrie, Juliet and Benjamin. So I got in touch and told them that I had just discovered I was Bob's daughter... and to my astonishment they already knew.

'I can't believe you've only just found out,' Juliet said, showing genuine surprise. 'Come and see us in London. We've got a lifetime of news to catch up on.'

I explained that I lived in the Dales, so she suggested spending a weekend at her country home in Northumberland.

It was May Day when I drove north to Alnwick with David, Rachel and my four-year-old great-granddaughter, Shara. As we drove up the farm track, the excitement of meeting my new-found cousins was tinged with apprehension. It was strange meeting new relations at my age. The house was the last of a group of converted farm buildings set in the middle of open countryside. We arrived to the sight of Carrie and Juliet sitting on the lawn with sun hats on, drinking tea, and some cows grazing in an adjoining field. It was a wonderfully pastoral English scene. We greeted each other as long-lost friends before Juliet went to fetch some refreshments and a rocking horse for Shara. Then we launched into conversation about Bob and memories of 1 Eaton Square.

Carrie recalled, 'I once spent Christmas there and complained that I never got a sixpence as I didn't like Christmas pudding. So Bob reached into his pocket and gave me half a crown, saying it would make up for all the Christmases I missed. That's how I remember him… so generous and kind.'

And as one story was told after another, I was reminded of Bob's fun-loving nature and enjoyment of giving.

As we went through to the kitchen, the house felt light and airy with an easy mix of traditional and contemporary furniture. The table was laid with a spread of local cheeses, salads, stuffed vine leaves, hummus and bread. As we lingered over lunch, Juliet mentioned that she had studied History of Art and now worked as a curator at Waddesdon Manor.

'Isn't that where Jacob Rothschild lives?' I asked.

'Yes, he's my boss,' she smiled.

I explained that Victor and Tess had been close friends of my parents and that I had known them all my life.

'I don't think Jacob and his father got on,' Juliet commented.

'They didn't,' I agreed. 'They fell out a long time ago and Jacob left the bank to set up on his own. I don't think their relationship ever healed. But Jacob always got on well with my mother, so please let him know that Bob is my father as he'll be much amused.'

Then I turned to Carrie to ask about her.

'Mine's a long story,' she smiled, 'and this weekend is about you.'

In the afternoon we went for a walk through woods and fields around the house, and Juliet mentioned that her father Simon had written his impressions of Bob. She explained that he was a psychologist and wanted to offer a deeper understanding of Bob's complex personality and lifestyle as he found the official biography too tailored. As Bob was Simon's godfather, they had kept in touch throughout his life.

'Was it published?' I asked.

'No... no one's read it apart from a few people in the family,' Juliet replied. 'I often wondered why he wrote it, but now I think it was for you. You and your sister are mentioned as being Bob's children.'

I stopped in my tracks and asked how the family knew.

'It was common knowledge,' Juliet explained. 'It seems it was only your parents who kept it secret. I can't believe they never told you.'

That evening Juliet gave me Simon's typewritten appraisal of Bob, warning me that he was not very complimentary about my mother.

She explained, 'I met your mother on several occasions at Eaton Square and remember her being quite forceful and domineering. My father obviously felt the same.'

So that night I sat in bed with Simon's thirty-page reminiscences of Bob. It began with an account of his bisexuality and went on to detail his numerous affairs, surmising what each had meant to him. Later, different aspects of Bob's personality were described – his courage, generosity, kindness, vanity, as well as his tendency to succumb to depression. I leafed through the first few pages quickly as I wanted to get to Simon's account of my mother – and there she was listed as one of Bob's lovers. He described her as being 'hard and controlling' and alluded to the deception she carried out in order to keep their affair secret. Finally Simon went on to explain that because of my mother's close friendship with Robert Rhodes James, Bob's biographer, she persuaded him not to mention her by name but sentimentalise their relationship.

> *When Bob was in Cambridge in the Royal Airforce, he met a woman of great attractiveness, high intelligence and sparkle. Immediately they were attracted to one another, which developed into a long, affectionate friendship that lasted to the end of his life.*

Simon also clearly resented the way that my mother took charge of Bob, organising his social engagements at Eaton Square and dictating who should and should not be invited. Simon ended the piece by saying:

> *Bob and Nora had two daughters called Teresa and Elizabeth.*

He wrote about Bob's other lovers, including Dorothy Macmillan, with whom he had a thirty-year affair. Although Bob described her as 'demanding, possessive and no great beauty', he was besotted by her as she was with him. Simon also had insights into her husband, Harold Macmillan, whom he compared with Dick, questioning what kind of a man tolerates his wife having a lifelong passion for someone else. But he went on to describe both husbands as being 'long-suffering and saintly', having to be strong within themselves to cope with their wives' ongoing infidelity.

Bob had other mistresses too, one of whom was Barbara Rothschild, Victor's first wife. I knew that Bob and Victor had at one time been close friends but had finally parted company, so maybe this was the reason. It seemed that Bob's dream was to have a house in the country and family of his own, but it was never to be. Instead he had a succession of affairs, some long lasting and others brief liaisons, and allowed his children to be brought up by other men.

As I lay my head on the pillow, different visual images of Bob, my true father, came and went – sitting in an armchair at Eaton Square in his pyjamas and dressing gown; dressed in a tweed suit wearing trousers Oxford-bag style, smoking a pipe; and turned out in a suit with a carnation in his lapel ready for an appearance at the House of Lords. I then took my mind to the many roles he played – lover of women and men, the entertainer, politician, rebel, man of courage and vision, the giver, the gambler, and one who dedicated his life to helping those less fortunate than himself. He found solace in music, poetry and the arts.

The following day we went to the beach. The sea was cold, but I went for a swim and dunked my head underwater. It felt like a baptism, a time of new beginnings, embracing my father and family that I had never known. With a gentle breeze blowing in from the sea, we walked along the cliffs to a fish restaurant, where Carrie treated us to lunch. There was an unstoppable flow of conversation and, as we talked, I noticed that my new relations expected nothing from me, I was accepted for who I was, and appreciated for having had the courage to find out the truth.

When I got home, I began reading the book that until then I had avoided, *The Peer and the Gangster*. My immediate feeling was one of gratitude to its author, Daniel Smith, who sensitively set Bob's association with the Krays in the context of his entire life. And there was one chapter, 'The Lost Boys', that gave me another insight into Bob. It told the story of how as a young man he had lost two of his dearest friends within a few years of each other. Henry, his first cousin, was like a brother to him but was shot dead at the end of the First World War shortly after he had enlisted. Apparently Henry was exceptionally gifted, destined to achieve high office and adored by everyone, so the news devastated the family, and especially Bob. For years he was unable to talk about his cousin as he felt the pain of his loss so deeply.

The second fatality occurred during Bob's first year at university.

While swimming in the River Isis, another dear friend, Michael Llewelyn Davies, mysteriously was sucked under the water and drowned. The two incidents made Bob aware of the precarious nature of existence. During World War I, while still at school, he had listened to the fatalities of ex-students read out weekly; and at Oxford, empty dining halls, libraries and lecture rooms served as a constant reminder of the extent of the tragedy that had swept across the land. Bob then realised that before him lay a choice. Either he could sink into depression or pour his energy into bringing back life and laughter into the Oxford colleges. He chose the latter and vowed to *live to the full, taste every last drop, and let nothing get in his way*, which he did with gusto, courage and a degree of recklessness too.

I now wanted to pay my own respects to Bob by visiting Rattray Head, the most easterly point in his constituency of Aberdeenshire, where his ashes had been thrown into the sea. This time I was not just accompanied by David, Rachel and Shara, but my daughter Charlotte, her partner Tim, and Jason my nephew. I imagined the coastline of Aberdeenshire having small coves, sandy beaches and quaint fishing villages, as I had seen in black and white photographs taken in the forties and fifties. But as we approached Peterhead, we were greeted by oil refineries and a harbour that was so large we had to drive around it. Ocean-going trawlers were anchored in different basins and the fish market was a vast factory, where the catch was sorted, auctioned off and then loaded onto wagons, ready to be taken to the continent. The fishermen of Peterhead, to whom Bob had given lifelong support, had turned the town into one of the most important fishing ports in Europe.

When we arrived at Rattray Head, the sun shone, rain clouds threatened and the wind gently lifted the sand from the dunes. A little way out to sea was the lighthouse. Enjoying the warmth of the sun on my face, I stood on the beach, closed my eyes and took my mind to the flotilla of fishing boats a mile offshore, where fishermen from Peterhead and Fraserburgh had paid their last respects to Bob and cast wreaths into the sea. A feeling of gratitude washed through me for Bob and all that he had done for the fishermen and farmers throughout his life. As we drove on north, we crossed Boothby Road, a further reminder of how much he had been valued here. And at our hotel, the owner reassured us that in Scotland, Bob would always be remembered for the good he had done, rather than gossip about his personal life.

Further north along the Moray Firth, the coastline became as I imagined it was in Bob's time, with cliffs, coves and small fishing villages, where family trawlers were still taken out. At Troup Head, we watched hundreds of gannets, guillemots, razorbills and kittiwakes swoop in and out from their cliff perches as they fed their young. We discovered beaches with rock archways and caves, deserted inlets with crystal-clear pools, and once again we braved the sea, which was somewhat colder than Northumberland. And in the evenings we lingered over meals of fish stew, trout and seafood… and I reminisced about Bob.

I talked about his vision – his belief that World War II could have been avoided if Neville Chamberlain's policy of appeasement had been stopped; Bob's empathy with those in the East End of London during the Blitz, who showed unstinting courage after each bombing raid; his affinity with farmers and fishermen who put food on our tables; belief in the importance of embracing opportunity and living life to the full; and his love of Wagner, Debussy and Elgar – and then we drank Bob's health.

Lastly, I wanted to find out about Bob's spiritual aspirations, or indeed if he had any. Bob was brought up in Scotland, where there was a strong puritanical code of morality among non-conformist churches. So it was hardly surprising that he reacted against the Church, believing Christ's teachings had become:

A religion of death rather than life, slavery to sin rather than emancipation from it, and a religion of suffering rather than joy.

Instead he chose to embrace the qualities of courage and loving kindness as being infallible recipes for life, accompanied by a sense of humour. As he wrote later in life:

I have found that compassion – the urge to diminish the sum of human suffering and to help those in difficulty, trouble and distress – brings the most abiding personal happiness. And between compassion and cruelty there can be no compromise.

On our way home, I began to see more resemblances between Bob and myself. There is a persistent curl in the front of my hair that I have struggled with since childhood and I notice Bob has a similar wave. My eyes are like his too. I receive compliments about my voice and know that Bob was famed for his. I enjoy wine and good food but, unlike Bob, I love cooking and creating new dishes in the kitchen. I am also not afraid to step out of line, hold a different viewpoint from others and I am not averse to taking risks. Reading his books, I also notice that we have a similar writing style. We are both drawn to helping others too.

But maybe the greatest resemblance between me and my father is that we both have a lifelong need to be loved. It drew Bob into countless relationships and me into an early marriage, followed by another two... but it also inspired my search for unconditional love and freedom.

The Nature of Loyalty

~

It was summer and still light when my mother put me to bed. At the time I must have been five years old. I heard voices in the garden so discreetly pulled back the curtain to see what was happening. The wisteria was encroaching over the window so I knew that I would not be seen. My father was standing by my mother on the lawn and very gently he put his arm around her waist, leaned towards her and gave her a peck on the cheek. I was taken aback as I had never seen them kiss before, hold hands or touch one another. I jumped up and down on the bed and said excitedly, 'Teresa, guess what. I've just seen Daddy kiss Mummy.'

And surprised by my outburst, she got up to look too.

It was a scene that I shall never forget as it revealed the genteel formality of my parents' relationship, one of respect and cordiality rather than emotional or physical intimacy. There was also another time when I had insight into how they interacted with each other. It was when I was a teenager and my parents took me on holiday to Italy. Dick loved visiting churches and art galleries, seeing the work of Botticelli, Michelangelo and frescoes of Giotto and Piero della Francesco. We stayed in guest houses in Florence, Sienna, Montepulciano, and Rome was our final destination. But finding our hotel in the capital city proved difficult. The roads were busy, one-way streets confusing and, despite my father's excellent navigation skills, he found it difficult to get his bearings. From behind the steering wheel, my mother's frustration soon erupted into anger and it was not long before she lost control. I shrank back and put my fingers in my ears. I could not bear the sound of my mother yelling at Dick when he was doing his best to give her directions. After a couple of wrong turns, she pulled up and refused to drive any further until my father had gone on foot to find the guesthouse. When he returned he guided us seamlessly to our destination.

That evening, supper was strained and afterwards there was no escape as owing to the expense of accommodation in the capital city, I had a camp bed in my parents' room. Disturbed by the row, I could not sleep and sat up in bed. Glancing over towards my parents' bed, it looked as though there was only one person there, but I had not heard anyone go out. Then I realised that their bodies were so closely intertwined, it was as if they were one. I did not know whether I was more surprised or shocked, as I had never seen this degree of intimacy before, especially with my parents. I lay down quickly, hoping I had not been seen, and wondered who had reached out to whom. If it were my mother, it would reveal an awareness that her temper had been misplaced and she wanted to apologise; if it were Dick, it would be a desire to forgive and forget. But whoever it was, I felt reassured that there was this degree of closeness between them as until then I had thought otherwise.

As a child I was aware that it was the rhythm and routine of the household that was reassuring. When Dick was home at the weekends, he gardened, listened to music, accompanied my mother to a drinks or dinner party that she had arranged, and on Sunday carved the joint with precision and care. As for my mother, she was conscientious about providing her family with three nutritious meals each day and undertook all her domestic chores with diligence. So how, I wondered, had she conducted a long-term affair alongside her duties to the family and household?

I assumed that Bob and my mother had met in 1943, when he was in the RAF and posted near Cambridge. I also recalled my mother saying that the Rothschilds had introduced them. At the time Bob's affair with Dorothy Macmillan had been going on for thirteen years with no foreseeable end in sight. He recounted that it began on a golf course in 1930 when Dorothy, then married to Harold Macmillan with three children, had thrust her hand into Bob's and told him how much she loved him. As her husband refused to give Dorothy a divorce, she vowed to continue the relationship regardless. And despite her possessive nature and excessive demands, Bob was captivated by her irrepressible spirit and professed how much he loved her.

However, his loyalties were divided. He realised the extent to which his personal life would be curtailed if he did not break away from her, yet at the same time felt emotionally bound to her. He made one attempt to leave by marrying her cousin Diana Cavendish, but Bob realised from the outset that he had made a terrible mistake. After two years, they agreed to divorce, but remained lifelong friends. From thereon, Bob found escape by having brief flirtations with wealthy American heiresses or unavailable women so that Dorothy would not be jealous.

So during the war, when Bob met a beautiful, vivacious and intelligent woman with similar interests who already had family commitments, the arrangement suited him perfectly. She would neither pose a threat to Dorothy nor encroach upon Bob's freedom, both of which were essential for his peace of mind. As for my mother, it seems that she fell helplessly in love with Bob, who opened up a new world for her.

And so this extraordinary quintet danced around each other for fifteen years or more – two married couples with Bob at the centre. Dorothy and her insatiable need for Bob's time and attention; my mother wanting sexual gratification, excitement and social and political stimulus; and two husbands, Harold Macmillan and Dick, both dedicated to keeping their marriages intact despite the behaviour of their wives. But they were different times. Divorce was frowned upon and the media respected personal privacy so did not intrude in the way they do now. Within the higher echelons of society, living a double life was not unusual, so the arrangement suited them well. Macmillan was ambitious and wanted to achieve high office, so maintaining a facade of respectability and keeping his marriage intact was crucial. And Dick's sense of honour and enduring love for Nora meant that he could neither face the humiliation of a failed marriage, nor bear the thought of losing her. As for Bob, at last had found a lover who was able to understand his feelings for Dorothy and accept that she would always be a part of his life.

But no relationship exists in isolation. There was the wider family to take into account. My maternal grandmother lived with my parents, but she would have kept silent even if she had suspected her daughter's infidelity. It was different with Dick's parents. My mother had the greatest respect for her parents-in-law and the last thing she would have wanted was to cause any upset within their family. So for this reason alone, she would have done all she could to keep her affair secret whatever deception was necessary, in order to maintain the illusion of David family harmony and contentment.

Fortunately for her, as Simon Carey had rightly perceived, Dick had sufficient inner strength and self-assurance to allow his wife to have her freedom without showing any signs of jealousy or resentment. He never failed to stand by her side when the storms swept in and make whatever sacrifices were necessary, including taking on two children who were not his.

I recalled him saying in his later years that he identified with the character of King Lear, who failed to recognise the steadfast love that his youngest daughter felt for him. Maybe now it was understandable that Dick found it difficult to relate emotionally to his two step-daughters and was happier pursuing his own interests instead. But having the courage to navigate the course he did, my mother was able to embrace two worlds – one in which she had emotional and sexual freedom, and another which allowed her to be a dutiful wife.

Her respect for Dick never waned. She admired his intellect, eclectic knowledge, understanding of music and the arts, and valued his political insights too. He was the rudder that kept her ship steady from the first time they met at university. She relied upon Dick in a multitude of ways, from doing her tax returns to writing and editing her speeches for the House of Lords. Without Dick's steadfastness, my mother might have lost her way, and without her gift for entertaining and bringing people together, Dick may have become a recluse.

In knowing the truth, my love and respect for both my mother and Dick deepened. My heart now went out to the person who I thought was my father but from whom I had felt emotionally distant for much of my life. I could also understand why Bob had taken care of Teresa and me, showing love and interest in us both as children and young adults. I respected my mother too for honouring Dick and standing by his side, despite being in love with another. But there was another who had taken me under his wing – namely Victor Rothschild. With respect to him, I knew that there was more to unravel.

A NEED TO CONTROL

~

For many the 3rd Lord Baron Victor Rothschild still remains a mystery, to his family as well as his closest friends. So I was drawn to find out about his different personas, his goals and aspirations for humanity and the world, and to what lengths he would go to achieve them.

Victor had a powerful presence and always commanded attention. With one penetrating look, he could invoke fear in others, whether it was Tess, his children, friends or colleagues, ensuring those around him danced to his tune so not to upset or anger him. But I never felt apprehensive around Victor, neither as a child nor an adult. On the contrary, he was one of the few people to whom I could express myself freely and openly. I could tease him, make him laugh, spar with him and discuss wild ideas to see where they led... something I could never have done with my own family. And in return I valued his incisive mind and help in finding solutions to any problem I faced in my life.

There was no right or wrong with Victor, just an endless line of enquiry, which allowed the two of us to probe and explore. He was like a father figure, doing his best to protect me from the storms that I weathered as a child. Early on, he recognised that I was a misfit in the academic world, but he never judged or thought less of me for it. He must have known that I was not Dick David's daughter as my mother would have shared her secret with Tess, her closest friend. Maybe this was why Victor showed compassion for the one who did not belong?

But it is easy to romanticise about the past and I was looking for truth. So I began reading the letters I received from Victor that I had found when looking through Bob's correspondence. Most of them were written in the early seventies, when we were seeing each other regularly at St James's Place. Some were handwritten and others typed, but all of them were signed off with a capital L and a V stroked through it – his abbreviation for 'Love Victor'. As I read them, I was moved by their tone and the care he showed. If days or weeks went by without hearing from me, he became concerned and feared something was amiss, aware that my relationship with Martin was volatile. There were also requests for me to call him if I had need of anything. In one letter he wrote:

I was lying in bed two nights ago and thought, 'if I hear that Biff is in trouble, I am immediately going to weigh in'.

As it happened I was in trouble; I called him and he said that he had sensed it. And that was how our relationship worked. We seemed to connect on another level. He picked up what I was feeling, so there was no need to hide anything. With Victor, I was able to be myself. And in return I accepted him for who he was, not judging or blaming him, despite knowing how ruthless he could be.

But in those days I had a rebellious streak in me too. It expressed itself through my poetry. I felt impatient with people who did not bother to question themselves, the nature of reality and our purpose here on this Earth. I became intolerant with those who were wedded to image and superficial values, and did not bother to draw back the veils to discover the potential that lies within us all. Victor felt the same and resonated with the first lines of one of my poems:

I'll follow the track
Onwards with the force of time
Tearing away the negative passivity
That indolence and ignorance instil...

It was a plea for everyone to stand for courage and truth instead of being cowed by fear... and Victor understood what I meant. As with my other poems, he always looked for the deeper meaning:

Your latest poem is really good. I understand more about you since reading it and realise how much there is to take from it... if one can.

I also found the letter Victor sent after I had torn up the cheque from Rothschilds Bank. As I remembered, he showed humility and apologised, expressing his sorrow for offending me and offering reassurance:

During the last ten or so years, I have from time to time thought you needed an ally and have tried, partially, to fill that role. I shall not interfere with you paddling your own canoe, but if you need a friend, I am always here.

So Victor became one of the few people to whom I could say, 'No,' as I knew he would not spurn me.

There were also letters that talked about the summer harvest at Rushbrooke, how his apple juice business was doing and inviting me to supper to celebrate his birthday. He said how much he enjoyed my company, poems and letters and always wanted to take an interest in what I was doing. Indeed, he was the only person within the Cambridge circle who was curious about meditation, wanting to know how it worked and whether it had a use in the wider world.

'Meditation is contrary to everything we experience in life,' I explained. 'It's not about doing, trying or having any goals. It's about allowing the mind to dive within so we can access the creative potential that lies within us all. It's easy to do but profoundly subtle.'

He replied, 'If it's a delicate process, I rather like those.'

As I looked through more letters, I kept pausing, feeling gratitude and appreciation for the role that Victor had played in my life. I also realised how much my move to the North had saddened him. He said that he missed our talks and times together, as I did too. But when I visited Cambridge, I made sure that I always saw him. More often than not it was over a drink, when the ritual of Victor asking me to sit beside him continued no matter who else was there. I then recalled the last time I saw him at the Garrick Club, when he told me how much our friendship had meant to him.

But now I wanted to find out about the side of Victor I had heard about but not directly experienced. I knew him as someone who could charm, entertain, be witty and curious, and with precision could cut through an argument to get to its crux. But it seemed there was another side that he kept hidden from his friends, family and colleagues too. Certainly I had seen the way he could treat his children, show contempt for a guest he did not tolerate, and impose his will on a person or situation with no concern for another's feelings. And although Tess was devoted to him, when she was with him she trod carefully and later in life confided that he held secrets to which she was not privy. So what were they?

When Victor was named as a contender for being the fifth man in the Cambridge spy ring, I was not surprised as I imagined that he might have been their controller. But if he was, what were his goals and aspirations, and how far did he go in realising them? The story began with his great-great-grandfather, Mayer Amschel Bauer.

Born in 1744 in Frankfurt, Mayer Amschel was a successful money lender, who was taken on by Prince William of Prussia as his personal banker. As Bauer's reputation grew, his influence spread, and, keen to amass more wealth, he sent his five sons to different European countries to further his ambitions. His eldest son, Nathan, came to Britain and wanting to elevate the family's status, changed the family name to Rothschild, meaning Red Shield. From then on, the five sons used duplicity, skill and ingenuity to ensure that the House of Rothschild profited from national and international disasters, enabling them to take control of the financial markets across the world and become the banking dynasty it is today. As Nathan Rothschild said:

> *I care not what puppet is placed upon the throne. It is the man who controls the money supply that controls the Empire – and I control that money supply.*

So to what extent did Victor follow in his ancestors' footsteps? He was a senior executive in NM Rothschild Bank and placed himself in strategic positions whereby he could move freely within government, intelligence agencies, scientific and nuclear research facilities, gleaning information and passing it on to those he chose. He also had the ear of a succession of British prime ministers, beginning with Winston Churchill in World War II. Aware of his many indulgences, Victor was able to bribe him with cigars, fine dining and introductions to the rich and famous, that allowed him to gain access to information and thereby become an influencer. The real winner of the war was the Rothschild Banking cartel, whose assets soared as they financed both sides.

As a child, I remembered Tess telling us about the Freemasons and their strange rituals involving ropes, swords and daggers. From Victor's days with the Apostles, he moved on to become a high-degree Freemason and, like others in prominent positions of power, used this as a way of networking and connecting with like-minded people. Within the Freemasons, the inner circle of initiates has access to sacred, arcane knowledge, which has been passed down through mystery schools for thousands of years. Such wisdom teachings can either be used to help free humanity spiritually or – when inverted – for its subjugation.

I knew of Victor's disdain for politicians and bureaucracy and admiration for those with brilliant and incisive minds. I was also aware of his idea that governance should be under the control of an intellectual elite, who would be able to manage humanity far more effectively and efficiently. So I began searching for leads.

My first clue came from a Russian journalist called Yuri Bezmenov who, in the 1960s, worked for a Soviet news agency. His job entailed spreading propaganda on behalf of the KGB and his government for the specific purpose of manipulating the perceptions of people both in Russia and the USA. Among Bezmenov's assignments, the KGB sent him to India to find out about Maharishi's technique of meditation. Aware that the practice was attracting the attention of those in the West, the Soviet government wanted to find out if it could be used to numb the population into a state of inert compliance. I remembered Victor wondering if meditation could be used by factory workers for the same purpose.

When Bezmenov realised that he was being used by his government to spread misinformation for the purpose of undermining Western democracies, he decided to defect. At great personal cost, he escaped to India, disguised himself as a hippie, acquired new documents and finally found refuge in Canada.

Bezmenov wanted to inform US intelligence that the Soviet Union was planning to impose a system of government known as 'collectivism' upon the Western world. This involved persuading people voluntarily to give up their individual rights and freedoms for the sake of 'the collective'. In this way a system of rule would be installed whereby the masses would be controlled by the few. But when Bezmenov approached the CIA and FBI to warn them of the impending threat, he was told it was too late as the groundwork for 'collectivism' was already in place. Aware of Victor's sympathies with Marxist-Leninist ideologies, along with his contacts in Russian, British and American intelligence, I presumed that Victor had played a part in this.

But I knew that I was scratching the surface and I wanted to uncover the truth, which all too often remains hidden behind official narrative and story. I remembered hearing the veteran journalist John Pilger warning that the mainstream media was now little more than a government propaganda machine and that we need to be sceptical about everything they report. Indeed, there were now very few journalists I trusted, but I found two.

One was a practising Jew, deeply committed to his faith, who had dedicated his life to making clear the distinction between the spiritual aspirations of his own people and the political aims of the Zionist movement. He had also done extensive research into the history and aims of the Rothschild family.

The second journalist was called Joachim, lived among the hills in Bali, and described himself as a 'die-hard truth seeker'. He had not only exposed international paedophile rings but also the intentions behind Russian, British and American intelligence during and after World War II. Amidst both journalists' substantial body of work were long, in-depth reports on Lord Victor Rothschild and his contacts, long-term goals, and his ability to by-pass governments to achieve his ends. After reading and researching different references, sources and official records, I was left in little doubt that Victor played a crucial role in subverting Western governments, with the view to putting in place a system of global control, based upon the idea of collectivism.

As Bezmenov explained, espionage as perceived in films and thrillers plays only a small part in the operations of those who work in intelligence. In order to impose fundamental change within society, the values and traditions of its culture have to be consistently undermined, which is achieved by infiltrating the political, legal, social systems and using education and the media to instil within communities the required message. By so doing, within a couple of decades, an entire generation can be indoctrinated and become the unwitting agents of their own culture's demise. As the journalist from Bali summarised:

> *We are governed, our minds are moulded, our tastes formed and our ideas suggested, largely by men we have never heard of. It is they who pull the wires that control the public mind. Those who manipulate this unseen mechanism of society constitute an invisible government, which is the true ruling power of our country and the world.*

So maybe Bob was right. Politicians hold little or no power and are simply servants of an unelected elite, who work through secret societies and non-governmental organisations to bring humanity under ever-increasing levels of global control.

But Victor's focus was not just on systems of government, but on how humans could be modified too. In his book *Meditations on a Broomstick*, he expressed the view that the process of evolution was too slow and needed to be accelerated by science. His field of research was the process of fertilisation, which inspired his interest in clones, eugenics and genetic engineering. I remembered him saying that it was only a matter of time before it would be possible to replicate humans and give them the characteristics required. He also mused about the development of a drug he called Extasin, which could be used to persuade people to conform, and another that would induce misery to punish those who did not. It seemed Victor saw humanity as a commodity that needed to be improved and modified as necessary.

I can never know what Victor's true intentions were, nor the lengths he went to achieve them, but I have little doubt that he was the spider at the centre of an invisible web, aspiring to put in place global government. So I mused that the depression at the end of

Victor's life may not have been because he was suspected of being the fifth man, but that he had been cast in a role that demeaned the truth of his life's work.

My personal experience of Victor, however, was of his empathy and understanding, so this is how I shall remember him. He was one of the few people who accepted me for who I was, and expected nothing of me. As a child he made me feel valued and understood. He never judged my failings but instead took the trouble to find out about me and my ideas. When I wrote about the sleeping masses being wedded to false reality, he understood what I meant. When I talked about specks of light that took form and travelled through different galaxies to the centre of the Universe, he sensed it might be true. He showed sympathy when I felt vulnerable, and had concern for my emotional and physical well-being. He also encouraged me to question, challenge and not take anything for granted, or on blind trust.

So I reflected upon what kind of conversation we might have now. As was his custom, there would be few words. But I sensed he would be pleased with the journey I have taken and glad that I had sought truth and found answers. With a pat on the back he might say, 'Well done, Biff. You saw behind the masks and were not taken in.'

Then I would ask him a question that had always mystified me, which was what was in the second package I brought back from Paris?

Victor and I both had a vision for humanity and the world, but his was secular and mine was spiritual. My journey entails accessing innate qualities that lie within us all so we can experience wisdom, truth and unconditional love and connect with the underlying unity of all. But Victor was drawn to explore the potential of the human intellect, gain temporal power and control, a pathway that is thwarted by limitation. By some Victor was called the King of the Jews for the role he played in the founding of the State of Israel. Mockingly, Yeshua's oppressors gave him the same title, but he reminded them that his Kingdom was not of this world... and Victor's was.

Conspiracy of Silence

~

From the moment I was conceived I was surrounded by deception. My mother had to cover her tracks, spin a story and pretend that I was the child of her husband just returned from the war, and not that of her lover of four years or more. But it was a familiar path. She had done it before. She had already convinced the family that Teresa was Dick's child, so she had little problem doing the same with me. When I was in her womb, an imprint of her feelings would have left its mark – guilt, shame and anger with herself for the situation she had created and the impact it had on others.

The lie became official as soon as I was born when, stamped upon my birth certificate, it was confirmed that I was the daughter of Richard William David, publisher of the Cambridge University Press. Dick now had two daughters and two sons – 'a brace of each', as Victor aptly put it, an occasion to celebrate. So the facade of a happy and united David family was portrayed to the world, while the dividing line between truth and deception became increasingly blurred.

The legacy of deceit leaves in its wake feelings of fear, doubt and uncertainty. As a child, I sensed that something was amiss. It was as if I did not belong, had done something wrong, that I was a misfit in the Cambridge world. Living alongside my family was like finding my way across quicksand, tentatively moving forward one step at a time, unsure if the ground would hold or whether I would sink in. My mother kept her walls of defence firmly in place, which maybe was why she was perceived as being hard and brazen. As Marni discovered, no one dared challenge her, neither her husband nor closest friends. So all my mother had to do was keep feelings at bay and let no chinks appear in her armour.

'I don't like emotionalism,' she would say. 'I like the company of those who make me laugh.'

Through laughter she could forget. She needed escape routes, which she found through socialising, partying, pursuing her political activities and fulfilling domestic duties with military precision. She could never rest or be still. Once she came to the Meditation Centre wondering if the practice would help her sleep. But when I asked my students to close their eyes, my mother pulled out a newspaper and rustled the pages as she read, much to the amusement of the others. At night she could not bear the silence so listened to the radio, and only turned it off when she got up the following morning.

When I asked my mother if Teresa was Bob's child, I would have imagined it would be a relief to share her secret and finally lay to rest her conflicted feelings. But all she did was to admit that Teresa 'could be,' and then deflect the question by talking about Sebastian. Yet this would also have been her chance to explain the irresistible attraction there had been between Bob and her, how much she loved him, that Dick had accepted it, and Teresa and I were the result. I sometimes wondered why my mother was so adamant about Teresa and I not speaking at Dick's funeral. But of course, she wanted to honour Dick's heritage by ensuring his two sons represented him and not his step-daughters. So my mother chose to take her secret to her grave, trusting that no flaw in the story would be found.

There was an unwritten agreement between Dick, Bob and my mother to keep the truth hidden by maintaining a conspiracy of silence. Maybe Dick convinced himself that he was beyond feelings of envy, but how did he feel when my mother stayed in London with Bob or went on trips with him abroad? And when Teresa and I called him 'Daddy', would there not have been a sense of regret that we were not his? It is little wonder that he was drawn to the Wagnerian themes of love and tragedy, the misfortunes of characters in a Shakespeare play, and faces in a Rembrandt painting that spoke to him. Friends wanted to reach out and offer support, but they were gently pushed aside. So Dick carried his burden alone and in silence.

It was different for Bob, as all he had to do was to watch his words when he was with the David family. Unconcerned by what others might think, he never felt it necessary to keep his love affairs secret, nor his relationship with Dorothy Macmillan. It seems that all his family knew that he had three illegitimate children by two different women and accepted it. Nor did Bob have a conscience about fostering his children out and allowing his mistresses' husbands to bring them up. By way of recompense, he offered financial help and bestowed generous gifts upon the families. But Bob did assume the role of father when he was with my mother, Teresa and me. After all, we were his family so he felt able to express his love for us freely. And although ignored, he was the only person who had the courage to tell Teresa the truth… that he was her real father – and mine too.

Bob may not have lied about his long and short-term affairs, but deception had no bounds when it came to safeguarding his public and political reputation. I was just sixteen when he took refuge in Cambridge after his name had been linked with the Krays. At the time I suspected he was not telling the truth, but now the full extent of the cover-up had come to light, which involved those at the highest level of government. Excuses could be made that Bob was approaching sixty, suffering from depression and increasingly relied upon alcohol and diversion to alleviate its effects. At the time, parties among the rich and famous were pushing the boundaries of conventionality, so maybe it was understandable that Bob succumbed to their temptations as a means of escape. Esmerelda's Bar in Knightsbridge with its new gaming licence was more accessible than Monte Carlo, and Bob was unconcerned that it was owned by the Krays, who cultivated the rich and famous to serve their own ends. So into their net he fell – the world of sex parties, protection rackets and crime.

The press was discreet about Bob's affairs, but having relationships with men when homosexuality was illegal and befriending East End gangsters was too juicy for them to ignore. Bob was accustomed to taking risks, but he was now playing a more dangerous game and the stakes were higher. Yet he held the trump card. Still reeling from the damage caused by the Profumo affair the year before, the political establishment could not afford another scandal to erupt so soon. Politicians on both sides of the House had become associated with the Krays, so Parliament would be disgraced and public confidence shattered once again if the story was allowed to break.

As a result it was agreed by the Prime Minister, Harold Wilson, the leader of the Opposition, law lords, the press and Metropolitan police to adopt a policy of silence and threaten anyone who revealed the truth. But one deception leads to another and the repercussions spread far and wide. Knowing the Kray twins were in possession of incriminating evidence, their silence had to be bought too, so the police were instructed to ignore their criminal activities, which allowed them to continue their reign of terror for another four years, effectively immune from prosecution.

Even when the twins were found guilty of murder and given life sentences, the government could still not rest easy as others knew the truth. The author John Pearson had spent years researching the Krays, Bob's friendship with them, and the government cover-up. So in 1969 when his book was about to go to press, Lord Goodman instructed MI5 to appropriate the script from the publisher and all incriminating evidence from Pearson's house, ensuring once again that the truth was suppressed.

It was Lord Goodman who also came to Victor Rothschild's rescue. When suspicions arose about him being the fifth man, the government could not risk another key member of the British establishment being exposed as a spy. Victor had been awarded the George Medal and American Legion of Merit for courage shown in World War II and was a valued and respected figure in public life. If it were revealed that he too had betrayed his country, all credibility in British intelligence would be lost. So the investigation was halted, resulting in Margaret Thatcher's announcement that the case against Victor Rothschild was 'closed on grounds of insufficient evidence'.

The same blanket of silence was cast over the deaths of three people connected to the Rothschild family. When Amschel was found dead in a hotel in Paris, despite French detectives saying they were at a murder scene, no investigation was allowed and the story was hushed up by the press.

The same happened after Olof Palme, Emma's lover, was shot dead in Stockholm. Despite Swedish people clamouring to know the reason for his untimely death, attempts to find the killer were frustrated by the authorities and to this day, neither a motive nor the assassin has been found. The same media and judicial silence prevailed after Miranda's husband was murdered too.

Increasingly a cloak of silence is being imposed upon us all, confusing and beguiling us, so we no longer know who or what to believe. Those who have the courage to challenge an established narrative are too often marginalised, dismissed or made to look a fool. But in exposing a secret that had blighted our family for so long, the truth had been revealed and the clouds of deception had gone – and I now saw myself, my family and the world in an entirely new light.

ANCESTRAL WOUNDS

~

I was born late evening on 12 November 1947, on a new moon and just before a solar eclipse. An Ayurvedic astrologer explained, 'The sun and moon are the two great luminaries. The sun represents the father and divine masculine, the moon the mother and divine feminine. At the time of your birth, the moon was debilitated, which was reflected in your conflicted relationship with your mother. But there was a purpose in this – to help you discover the mother and divine feminine within yourself.'

'And what about my father?' I asked.

'The sun was eclipsed, so your father was too. Your real father never made himself known to you and your step-father remained distant and aloof. But once again, this was your stimulus to find the divine masculine within yourself and bring it into perfect balance with the divine feminine. What a challenge you took on, but one day you will see its perfection.'

As I was familiar with Eastern traditions I knew about different ideas of rebirth and reincarnation, so I had no difficulty accepting that I had chosen the circumstances of my birth to accelerate my soul's growth. As an adult, I harboured no bitterness or resentment about my parents, nor what I had experienced as a child. Indeed, I just felt gratitude for all that I lived through and knew it had been the driving force behind my spiritual search. But in light of the revelation about my true paternity, I sensed that further healing was required.

I had heard from wisdom teachers that if one person in a family lineage is able to heal themselves, it not only benefits their ancestors but those who come after too – and Padma had intimated that this responsibility now rested with me. So what could I do? I assumed that the three pebbles Padma had seen in Yeshua's hand were the three betrayals associated with Bob's illegitimate children – but these were now exposed and the truth was out. I then recalled the block that Padma had seen at the back of my heart, which I recognised as fear that had undermined me for so long.

I had spent fifty years pursuing a spiritual path that had entailed plumbing the depths of myself to unearth my deepest wounds and understand how they expressed themselves. My sense of lack, worthlessness, was now much diminished, but I knew that vestiges still remained. This revealed itself when I blamed others for my own failings, used self-justification as a means of defence, or resorted to appeasement when I felt threatened or attacked... and I still feared rejection too. So now it was time for ruthless honesty, to face those parts of myself that I still avoided or denied. It was usually shock or trauma that prompted me to take a more discerning look at myself, but now it was an all-consuming desire to remove any obstacle that prevented me from coming into alignment with truth and love.

I closed my eyes and took my attention to my heart. Almost immediately I felt a fluttering of anxiety, so I put my hand there for reassurance. Then I became aware of a knot in my stomach, serving as a reminder that underlying fear was still present. As I went deeper I recognised that it bore the usual hallmarks – fear of criticism and the withdrawal of love by someone close to me.

I asked for more to be revealed and saw an image of a young girl lying huddled on the floor and a woman standing over her hitting her.

Part of me wanted to go and rescue the child, but I was frozen to the spot. My resistance surprised me as I felt sorry for the child, but at the same time there was contempt for allowing herself to be treated in this way. Maybe she deserved the punishment that was being inflicted upon her? I tried to banish the image from my mind but instead it became more intense, which made me look more closely. And as I did, I realised that both the mother and the child were me.

I had taken on the role of my mother. Just as she had rebuked me, I now did the same to myself. It was true that I still berated myself for mistakes I made, for not coming up to the mark, for my perceived failures, despite spending years assuring myself that I had done nothing wrong. So impressions from my past were still active, linking me to my ancestors and my descendants too.

While travelling in Buddhist countries in the East I had seen beautiful, ornate prayer wheels standing in pride of place in the front of people's houses. When I asked what they were for, I was told that a family member turned them each day in memory of the ancestors. In this way, those alive were reassured that they were being cared for and guided by those who had gone before them. Although in Western culture this tradition had been lost, I presumed it was no different for me. By taking my attention to the ancestors, a connection would be made.

Certainly since discovering that Bob was my father, I felt his presence around me and that of his parents too, glad that I had brought truth to the family line at last. I also knew about the trauma his family had experienced – the loss of loved ones in two World Wars, grief owing to premature death, betrayals and veils of secrecy drawn over events that no one wanted to face. And I now realised that Bob carried a similar wound to me – a profound need to be loved. His parents had showered him with love, but in adulthood this left a hole that Bob found difficult to fill. And within me, the same need had arisen from feeling deprived of love.

But as a woman with three daughters, I wanted to connect with my maternal ancestral line to see what patterns I had inherited through them. As my grandmother lived with us in Cambridge, I was familiar with her traits and idiosyncrasies. As a young woman she was spirited, but she married a man much older than herself, lost her two-year-old daughter to illness and was left a widow in her fifties. My mother described her father as a strict disciplinarian, who had a temper and cut her out of his will when she returned home late after an evening out. He was also secretive about his business dealings, sometimes making money and other times losing it, but always concealing the truth of their finances from my grandmother.

It was easy to see the patterns repeating themselves. My grandfather's need for control, his anger and need to deceive were all evident in my mother. My mother could also ride roughshod over my grandmother who was more like me, someone who avoided conflict and preferred to acquiesce rather than answer back.

I then turned my attention to my three daughters. As teenagers, I had seen defiance and compliance in them all as they found their independence, discovered their gifts and decided how best to use them. But my concern had always been Rachel and Abi's relationship with their father... or lack of it. Having moved to the Dales when they were young, they had scarcely seen him apart from brief visits to London, where they weathered his fluctuating moods.

Over the years, I had done what I could to compensate for their father's absence, but I knew that there was no replacement for a loving, attentive father. As Padma had warned, patterns not only repeat themselves through the generations but also intensify. My great-granddaughter Shara does not even know who her father is.

'Where is my papi?' she asks, and there is no answer.

And so the wound of abandonment carries on.

Wanting more insight as to what more I could do to help, I took myself off to sit by the river, where all was peaceful and calm. Feeling the warmth of the sun on my face, I allowed my mind to drift and a succession of scenes came and went... but there was one that made me shudder. I was in Cornwall with Rachel as a young girl, and Abi an infant in her pushchair. We were walking across a field, and out of the blue, Rachel had a tantrum and ran off towards a precipitous sea cliff, oblivious to the danger that lay ahead. I panicked and ran after her, leaving Abi alone in the middle of the field. At one point I looked back and saw her crying, waving at me, bewildered as to why her mother was leaving her. Torn apart by the needs of my two daughters, I realised that I could not protect them both. And as I relived this moment, I remembered the countless times I believed I had failed them, always blaming myself for any hardship they encountered.

On one level I was able to let them go, whether it was physically to the other side of the world or emotionally to a chosen partner. But I had always felt their happiness was my responsibility. Their pain became my pain and I could not bear to see them suffer.

But as I recalled the scene on the Cornish cliff – grabbing Rachel just in time, her breaking down in tears and then us running back to Abi – a deeper letting go occurred, a knowingness that it was not my place to save them or divert them from their path. We all have the gift of free will and it is only by facing our own difficulties that we learn the lessons we need and are able to move on. Life experience had been my teacher and it was no different for my children.

Indeed, I now blessed every circumstance that came my way and bore no grudge against those who challenged me. Without them I would not be the woman I am today. So all I could do for my children was surround them with love, knowing at times that they would stumble and fall, and only if they reached out for help would I be there to support them. As my perspective changed, instead of focussing on their behaviours, I saw in them qualities that were unchanging – their courage, appreciation and joy.

With this realisation, I felt a softening around my heart, followed by an expansion beyond my physical form. I could now see that fear is illusory, born of the ego and not of the heart, where only love resides. Feelings of gratitude welled up along with a sense of profound trust that all would be well, each one of us cared for in ways that we cannot tell.

The image of the child returned, but this time no one was hitting her. Without hesitation I gathered her up in my arms. She was smiling, beautiful and radiant. Holding her close, I stroked her soft brown hair, reassuring her that she had never done anything wrong and that I would not abandon her again. As the tears flowed the image of the girl faded but I felt her vibration within.

Sometimes I feel her in my heart, but other times she is away, dancing on the treetops, flying with the swallows or merging with the water that flows in the streams. She is a sprite, a light being, visible only to those who can see. She is the epitome of love and all that I long to be.

The Portal of Truth

~

'First one to see the sea,' I cried out excitedly as my mother drove along the last stretch of road to the house in Cornwall.

But I was never the one who saw it first. I was too small and until we were almost at the house, it could only be glimpsed above the windswept hedges. As David and I made the journey seventy years later, we played the same game, and again it was he who saw it first just beyond the village of Delabole.

This time it felt strange returning to the place where I had spent my childhood summers. My sister had sold the family home to a developer and had warned me that it had now been demolished and replaced by a five-bedroomed, steel-framed dwelling. When we arrived, we fortified ourselves with a Cornish pasty and cider before doing the familiar walk across the beach. The sun was shining, a fresh wind was blowing in from the sea and the waves rolled in with an evenness I had rarely seen.

As we approached the house along Sandy Lane, my first shock was seeing a bank of manicured turf where once there had been a garden with indigenous flowers, shrubs and a wooden bench overlooking the bay. I then turned to the house, which I had difficultly recognising. Its gently sloping slate roofs, porches and verandahs had been replaced by the hardness of fabricated steel, floor-to-ceiling glass with a box-like room built onto the roof. The cyclamen, primroses, rosemary and thyme had gone in favour of a driveway. And the lawn where we played French cricket, shelled crabs and ate saffron cake had been rooted up and replaced by white tiles that dazzled in the midday sun.

A builder introduced himself as the site manager, so I explained that my family had owned the house and I had known it all my life.

'The new build has gone up in less than five months,' he said proudly. 'Electric point for the car, air source heat pump, multiple layers of insulation and five bedrooms, all ensuite.'

He offered to show us around, explaining that the stairs had only just been varnished, so we would not be able to see the master bedroom on the roof. As I crossed the threshold, it was clear that all vestiges of the place I had spent my childhood days had gone. The character and style of the seaside home had been replaced by abrupt, angular lines, creating an impression of efficiency and functionality rather than beauty, ease and grace. In place of the window seat, where generations of adults and children had watched the sea and sunsets, were now featureless panes of glass, and off to one side a modern kitchen that to me looked like a laboratory.

As I tried to reorient myself, memories came flooding back of the days when my mother had used the pantry to store food and stood milk in buckets of cold water on the floor. Suddenly I had an urge to leave, so I thanked our guide, took David's hand and hurried off down the path that led to the cliffs.

It was a relief to get up high and watch the waves breaking on the rocks. At least the landscape had not changed, apart from more pebbles being washed up at Cowrie Bay that raised the level of the beach. No longer would it be possible to dive in from the rocks as we had done as children. We walked on to a headland, where my grandmother spent hours watching sea birds and the view. As soon as we arrived, a seal popped up in the bay one hundred feet below, followed by another and then two pups. We called out to them to hold their attention and, intrigued by the sound, they stayed for a while. Then suddenly they disappeared, the light changed and the sea gave off a luminous blue green light that rose up and enveloped us, making everything feel unworldly.

The following day, we visited St Enedoc's Church, famed for its leaning spire owing to the chapel having once been buried in sand. We were welcomed by the warden, who asked where we were from, so I mentioned the fate of our family home.

'There's a microwave oven going up next to us too,' he said. 'Pack in the guests and make as much money as you can is the philosophy now. It's happening everywhere.'

I sympathised, settled myself in a pew and recalled the time when Dick's parents had sat on Rabbit Hill, wondering if they could afford to buy the seaside home. An image of Gran came to mind that was so clear it was as though she was with me. She was sitting in a deck chair on the verandah, hands folded in her lap, with her hair drawn back in a bun just as I remembered her. I wanted to express my sympathy about what had happened to the family home, but she was quite still, seemingly beyond emotion, radiating an aura of dignity.

It was as though she was aware of everything that was happening now, and in both the past and the future, reassuring me that all was well. Then by her side I noticed Dick, my mother, Bob, their parents and gathering behind them was my entire ancestral lineage, each one reaching out to me, my children and their children too. I could feel the power of their presence around me, but I knew there was more to be revealed. I returned my gaze to Gran, but she had changed. No longer was she the woman I knew, but a symbol of Truth, immutable and unchanging.

As I left the church, the word 'truth' remained emblazoned across my mind. I knew that this was not a concept or an idea but a direct experience that lay within, only to be found when we had opened to our fragility, vulnerability and healed our wounds through loving embrace. It seemed my ancestors wanted to show me a higher expression of truth, so as I lay my head on the pillow that night, I asked for more guidance and an answer came in a dream.

I was in a war-torn, ravaged country, moving among buildings that had been bombed out of all recognition. There were remnants of shells littering the streets, dead bodies, orphans looking for food or a hand to hold. An occasional person appeared from behind a pile of rubble, lost and confused, rummaging through the debris looking for some memory of their past. Neither safety, shelter nor water were anywhere to be found. People were covering their faces, either because of the stench in the air or the horror of what humanity is capable of inflicting on its own kind.

As I mourned the loss and devastation, suddenly I was lifted above it all and transported to a desert. Below there were huddles of people clutching a few belongings in the midst of a vast expanse of sand, with no reprieve from the midday sun. But almost as soon as the image came, it changed into another – a tropical forest that extended as far as the eye could see that was lush, bountiful and abundant. In a clearing there were some wooden houses, children laughing, women gathering nuts and seeds from the trees and storing them in wicker baskets. And close by there was a river, where men were fishing and building boats.

Then the trees, branches and foliage suddenly metamorphosed into high-rise office buildings, with no plant or flower in sight, where robotic, lifeless men and women were operating row upon row of computers attached to vast screens. I recognised them as our controllers who had taken over the world, programming and directing the activities of humans, whose only purpose now was to serve them.

Then all at once I was back in the Dales again looking for my home. But everything had changed. Where once my house had been, there was an underground warren of interlinking rooms with no windows to let in light and fresh air. As I was looking for a way out, the scene changed again, into a house by the sea that was spacious and inviting. Entranced by its beauty, I believed I had found my perfect home, but then a builder came to warn me that the walls were crumbling, the house was unsafe, so I had to leave.

At that point I thought I had woken up, but no. I was in yet another reality, but this one felt real and true. People from different cultures, countries and backgrounds were gathering together to build a centre that was to be a symbol of Truth and Love. There was excitement in the air, with each person offering their skills and ingenuity to realise this dream on Earth. A kaleidoscope of colours, sacred geometries, crystals, and fabrics soft as silk, came together in a dance of creation that took my breath away. As I marvelled at what I was seeing, a woman's face appeared, possibly of native American Indian origin, painted and decorated with jewels and beads.

As I was admiring her beauty, she spoke. 'You will not find what you are looking for here.'

'But it's a centre where people can experience eternal truths,' I explained.

'This too is an illusion. Look more closely.'

As I did, I was able to see beneath the surface, beyond what appeared to be real. Each person carried wounds no different from mine, and like me was conditioned by the behaviours that arose from them. They all had an agenda of their own, seeking from others the qualities and resources they lacked within themselves. As more veils were swept aside, I saw again how easy it is to be beguiled and deceived.

I looked at the wise woman again. 'So where is Truth to be found?'

And with a smile of reassurance, she disappeared.

When I awoke, the woman was still with me. I recalled the dream and wondered about my own journey. It now seemed like a fleeting experience, a sequence of scenes that made up a play that seemingly had no ending. As I reflected upon what had spurred my search for truth, two words cried out: 'suffering' and 'pain'. Indeed, from the time in my highchair when my mother wanted me to eat a cold, burned egg, a silent determination built up in me to right the wrong and seek justice.

But I had no idea what this journey would entail, nor the degree of courage and humility that would be needed. I now know the quest for truth comes at a cost. It involves treading a precarious pathway that requires us stripping away all pretence, so we are left naked, exposed, with no guises or masks to hide behind. Only when we become vulnerable are we able to receive. Then like a butterfly alighting upon a flower, Truth reveals itself as a gift of Grace.

All I had to do was to be still and wait in silent expectancy for Truth's call. It is ever-present, breathing through us every moment but can only be experienced when all our filters and distortions have gone. Truth cannot be defined, described or explained. It arises spontaneously from an open heart and, like universal love, allows us to connect with everything and everyone around. Truth whispers to us through the sound of water flowing over pebbles in a riverbed, the fragrance of a jasmine flower and the dexterity of a swallow's flight. It sings in our hearts as joy, appreciation and gratitude for all that we are offered in life. My mind had been opened, enabling me to see that beyond the illusion we are all One.

For thousands of years, mystics and seers have told us that this world is not our true reality. It is but a passing dream, a sketchbook of momentary experiences in which we adopt different roles, weave stories and get lost in the illusion of the five-sense world. I remembered Victor asking us the colour of the sea and it was then that I realised that nothing is as it seems. Now the clouds of confusion have dispersed, it is time to embark upon another journey, one in which nothing is certain and anything is possible.

No longer do I take on trust the endless narratives we are taught or told. I want to discover our origins, our reason for being, and the truth of our destiny in this three-dimensional world. Men and women genetically identical to ourselves lived on this planet two hundred thousand years ago, so what happened in all those intervening years? It is known that civilisations far more advanced than our own drew upon wisdom held in sound, water, crystals and minerals, and people resonated at a higher frequency that we do now. But periodically, when humanity is no longer in alignment with divine and natural law, civilisations implode and we have to begin all over again. In the history of our planet, once called the Blue Pearl, races have come and gone, empires risen and fallen, and visionaries say that there is a danger of this happening again.

I recalled when my father, who is no longer my father, woke me in the night to show me the pillars of green, yellow and white light spiralling up above Rabbit Hill. Now, on a clear winter night, I can sometimes see the faint plumes of the aurora borealis beckoning me on. The ancients spoke of a land beyond the North wind where the key to inner mysteries is held. Plato described it as the centre of the world, the Hindus called it Mount Meru, but it is also known as the Garden of Eden where the Tree of Knowledge radiates wisdom to humanity and the world. But only the intrepid venture to these lands as it is a pathless path and there is no map or compass. So a new adventure begins… into unknown, uncharted territory, where Truth and Love will be my guides.

Epilogue

~

As my story ends, I am drawn to go up the fell behind our house and connect with the woman I knew as Gran. It is a beautiful autumn day and the sky is vivid blue. As I climb, I pause every now and again to look back down Dentdale. I have always believed it to be a sacred place.

When I reach the top I sit on the cairn and allow my gaze to drift across the hills. Then I close my eyes and take my attention to Dick's mother. But all I can detect is her soft outline before she retreats into a mist and disappears. Now truth has been brought to her ancestral line, it seems that healing is complete.

Then unexpectedly I see my mother reaching out to me, bearing gifts of wildflowers. She is young, beautiful and appears to be offering me protection, reassuring me how much I am loved and that I will always be taken care of. But as I look more closely, I realise within my mother there is another – an expression of compassion and unconditional love. It is the Divine Mother taking the form of my mother so that I may recognise her. Her gentleness surrounds me, Her beauty captivates me and I am smiling, knowing She is always there for me.

The perfection of my journey now reveals itself – every event, relationship, the play of circumstance, all holding keys to help me realise the truth of who I am. No longer do I feel trapped within the dream but like a child again, innocent, enquiring, without fear holding me back.

As I make my way down the fell, I break into a run and feel the wind on my face. I am excited, curious, not knowing what the future holds. It is a mystery, unfolding moment by moment... and all I need do is respond to its call.

About the Author

Eliza has explored different spiritual pathways in both the East and the West and has been a teacher of meditation all her adult life. Alongside her work as a spiritual mentor and guide, she is also a photographer and author and has documented the life and landscape of Northern England through a series of illustrated books.

In 1997 Eliza wrote her autobiography *In Search of Freedom*, which led to her founding a meditation centre in the Yorkshire Dales. In 2013 she gave up her role as Director to research her first novel *The Mystery of Martha*, which was published in 2019. With her husband David, she now runs Sacred Meditation from their home in Cumbria.

www.sacredmeditation.com